Living Language™

CONVERSATIONAL
RUSSIAN

REVISED AND UPDATED

The Living Language™ Series

Living Language ™ Complete Courses, Revised & Updated

French*
German*
Inglés/English for Spanish Speakers
Italian*
Japanese*

Portuguese (Brazilian)
Portuguese (Continental)
Russian
Spanish*

*Also available on Compact Disc

Living Language ™ Complete Courses

Advanced French
Advanced Spanish
Children's French
Children's Spanish
English for Chinese Speakers

English for French Speakers
English for German Speakers
English for Italian Speakers
Hebrew

Living Language In-Tense ™ Verb Practice

French, German, Italian, Spanish

Living Language Plus®

French, German, Italian, Spanish

Living Language Traveltalk ™

French, German, Italian, Japanese
Portuguese, Russian, Spanish

Living Language ™ Speak Up!® Accent Elimination Courses

American Regional
Spanish
Asian, Indian, and Middle Eastern

Living Language ™ Fast & Easy

Arabic
Czech
French
German
Hebrew
Hungarian
Inglés/English
   for Spanish Speakers

Italian
Japanese
Korean
Mandarin Chinese
Polish
Portuguese
Russian
Spanish

Living Language™

CONVERSATIONAL
RUSSIAN

REVISED AND UPDATED

Revised by Nadya L. Peterson, Ph.D.
Assistant Professor of Russian
University of Pennsylvania

Based on the original
by Aron Pressman

CROWN PUBLISHERS, INC., NEW YORK

This work was previously published under the titles *Conversation Manual Russian* and Living Language™ *Conversational Russian* by Aron Pressman.

Published by Crown Publishers, Inc., 201 East 50th Street, New York, New York 10022. Member of the Crown Publishing Group. Random House, Inc. New York, Toronto, London, Sydney, Auckland.

LIVING LANGUAGE and colophon are trademarks of Crown Publishers, Inc.

Library of Congress Catalog Card Number: 58-12894

ISBN 0-517-59054-9

1993 Revised and Updated Edition

Manufactured in the United States of America

10   9   8   7   6   5   4   3   2

CONTENTS

INTRODUCTION

Living Language™ Conversational Russian makes it easy to learn how to speak, read and write Russian. This course is a thoroughly revised and updated version of *Living Russian: The Complete Living Language Course®*. The same highly effective method of language instruction is still used, but the content has been updated to reflect modern usage, and the format has been clarified. In this course, the basic elements of the language have been carefully selected and condensed into forty short lessons. If you can study about thirty minutes a day, you can master this course and learn to speak Russian in a few weeks.

You'll learn Russian the way you learned English, starting with simple words and progressing to more complex phrases. Just listen and repeat after the native instructors on the recordings. To help you immerse yourself in the language, you'll hear only Russian spoken. Hear it, say it, absorb it through use and repetition.

This *Living Language™ Conversational Russian* manual provides English translations and brief explanations for each lesson. The first seven lessons cover pronunciation, laying the foundation for learning the vocabulary, phrases, and grammar, which are explained in the later chapters. If you already know a little Russian, you can use the book as a phrase book and reference. In addition to the forty lessons, there is a Summary of Russian Grammar, plus verb conjugations and a section on writing letters.

Also included in the course package is the *Living Language™ Russian Dictionary*. It contains more than 15,000 entries, with many of the definitions illustrated by phrases and idiomatic expressions.

The most essential words are set off with an * at their side to make them easy to find. You can increase your vocabulary and range of expression just by browsing through the dictionary.

Practice your Russian as much as possible. Even if you can't manage a trip abroad, watching Russian movies, reading Russian magazines, eating at Russian restaurants, and talking with Russian-speaking friends are enjoyable ways to help reinforce what you have learned with *Living Language*™ *Conversational Russian*. Now, let's begin.

The following instructions will tell you what to do. Ни пу́ха, ни пера́! Good luck!

COURSE MATERIAL

1. Two 90-minute cassettes.

2. *Living Language*™ *Conversational Russian* manual. This book is designed for use with the recorded lessons, but it may also be used alone as a reference. It contains the following sections:

Basic Russian in 40 lessons
Summary of Russian Grammar
Verb conjugations
Letter writing

3. *Living Language*™ *Russian Dictionary*. The Russian/English-English/Russian dictionary contains more than 15,000 entries. Phrases and idiomatic expressions illustrate many of the definitions. The most essential words are set off with an * at their side.

INSTRUCTIONS

1. Look at page 2. The words in **boldface** type are the ones you will hear on the recording.

2. Now read Lesson 1 all the way through. Note the points to listen for when you play the recording. The first word you will hear is **Алекса́ндр** (Alexander).

3. Start the recording, listen carefully, and say the words aloud in the pauses provided. Go through the lesson once, and don't worry if you can't pronounce everything correctly the first time around. Try it again and keep repeating the lesson until you are comfortable with it. The more often you listen and repeat, the longer you will remember the material.

4. Now go on to the next lesson. If you take a break between lessons, it's always good to review the previous lesson before starting on a new one.

5. In the manual, there are two kinds of quizzes. With matching quizzes you must select the English translation of the Russian sentence. The other type requires you to fill in the blanks with the correct Russian word. If you make any mistakes, reread the section.

6. Even after you have finished the forty lessons and achieved a perfect score on the Final Quiz, keep practicing your Russian by listening to the recordings and speaking with Russian-speaking friends. For further study, try *Living Language Traveltalk*™ *Russian*.

Living Language™

CONVERSATIONAL
RUSSIAN

REVISED AND UPDATED

RUSSIAN

REVISED AND UPDATED

LESSON 1

A. THE LETTERS AND SOUNDS OF THE RUSSIAN LANGUAGE

Listen, then repeat. Russian pronunciation will be easy once you learn the rules of pronunciation and reading, which hold true with very few exceptions. It is just as easy to say *ah* as it is to say *oh*, or to say *vast* as it is to say *fast*. But if you pronounce *f* where it should be *v*, or *oh* where it should be *ah*, or *eh* where it should be *ee*, you will speak with a foreign accent. Knowing these rules will help you to have a sound picture of the word you are learning and will help you to recognize it when it is spoken by the native; you want to understand as well as to speak!

Russian is *not* phonetic. You *don't* read it the way it is spelled. Many native Russians think they do; most of them are sure they do—they are wrong!

Learn word units. Always try to pronounce pronoun, preposition, and adjective together with the word they modify. Note that all words that have more than one syllable are marked with an accent mark. This is done only for the sake of the student. Accent marks will not be found in reading material outside of textbooks, but for the sake of proper pronunciation, it is necessary to memorize the stress in each word.

Russian punctuation varies little from that of English in the use of the semi-colon, colon, exclamation point, question mark, and period. However, the use of the comma is determined by concrete grammatical rules and generally does not, as in English, indicate a voice stop.

Remember that the Russian language is not phonetic. Each letter represents several sounds. It is important to learn that at the beginning of your study and to acquire the proper speech habits at the very start.

The Russian language has twenty consonant letters representing thirty-five consonant sounds, since fifteen of these twenty letters can represent either soft or hard (palatalized or nonpalatalized) sounds. Three are hard only; two are soft only. There are ten vowels and one semi-vowel.

Softness, or palatalization, of consonants is indicated by the vowels: **е, ё, и, ю, я,** and **ь** (soft sign). When a consonant is followed by one of these vowels, the consonant is palatalized, i.e., it is soft. In palatalization, the articulation of a consonant in its alphabet (nonpalatalized) form is altered in a specific way: the place and manner of articulation remain the same, but the middle part of the speaker's tongue moves up to the palate to produce "palatalization." Palatalization in the Russian language has particular significance and should therefore be carefully studied, as the meaning of a word can be changed through palatalization. Listen carefully and try to imitate.

The alphabet is given in Lesson 3, but listening to the tape and looking at the spelling of the following names and words will help you to recognize the different sounds each letter can represent.

B. Names

Many Russian sounds are like English. Listen to and repeat the following Russian names and notice which sounds are similar and which are different:

Алекса́ндр	Alexander
Алексе́й	Alexis

Антóн	Anthony
Борúс	Boris
Валентúн	Valentine
Варвáра	Barbara
Вúктор	Victor
Владúмир	Vladimir
Волóдя	Volodya, dim. of Vladimir
Геóргий	George
Давúд	David
Димúтрий	Dimitri
Евгéний	Eugene
Екатерúна	Catherine
Елéна	Helen
Елизавéта	Elizabeth
Жéня	Gene, dim. of Eugene or Eugenia
Захáр	Zachary
Ивáн	John, Ivan
Игорь	Igor
Ирúна	Irene
Кáтя	Kate, dim. of Catherine
Кóля	Kolya, dim. of Nicholas
Константúн	Constantine
Леонúд	Leonid
Лúза	Liza, dim. of Elizabeth
Любóвь	Amy
Люба	dim. of Amy
Людмúла	Ludmilla
Максúм	Maxim
Маргарúта	Margaret
Михаúл	Michael
Надéжда	Nadezhda
Нáдя	Nadya, dim. of Nadezhda Nadine
Натáлия	Natalie

Ната́ша	Natasha, dim. of Natalie
Никола́й	Nicholas
О́льга	Olga
Па́вел	Paul
Пётр	Peter
Серге́й	Sergei
Фёдор	Theodore

NOTICE

1. that each vowel is pronounced clearly, but the same letter does not always have the same sound. This is especially true of the letter *o*, which sometimes has the sound of *oh* but more often the sound of *ah*. The letter *e* sometimes has the sound of *eh* and sometimes the sound of *ee*.

2. that the accent mark (´) shows the syllable that is stressed. The stressed vowel is pronounced in its alphabet form, with more emphasis (slightly longer and louder).

3. that each word has but one stressed syllable.

4. that stress in the Russian language follows no rule. Any syllable can be stressed.

5. that all syllables after the stressed syllable are pronounced with less emphasis.

Pay attention to the consonant and its palatalization.

C. Geographical Names

Австра́лия	Australia
А́зия	Asia
Аме́рика	America
Аргенти́на	Argentina
Арха́нгельск	Arkhangelsk
Байка́л	Baikal (Lake)
Баку́	Baku
Болга́рия	Bulgaria
Варша́ва	Warsaw
Вашингто́н	Washington
Великобрита́ния	Great Britain

Владивосто́к	Vladivostok
Во́лга	Volga
Гали́ция	Galicia
Герма́ния	Germany
Гру́зия	Georgia
Днепр	Dnieper
Дуна́й	Danube
Евро́па	Europe
Еги́пет	Egypt
Индия	India
Ита́лия	Italy
Ирты́ш	Irtisch (River)
Кавка́з	Caucasus
Калифо́рния	California
Ки́ев	Kiev
Константино́поль	Constantinople
Крым	Crimea
Македо́ния	Macedonia
Ме́ксика	Mexico
Москва́	Moscow
Нева́	Neva
Оде́сса	Odessa
Ока́	Oka
Псков	Pskov
Росси́я	Russia
Ряза́нь	Ryazan
Сама́ра	Samara
Севасто́поль	Sevastopol

LESSON 2

A. COGNATES: WORDS SIMILAR IN RUSSIAN AND ENGLISH

Listen to these Russian words, which are general equivalents of English words. These words are descended from the same root and are called cognates. Note the character of Russian pronunciation as well as Russian intonation.

абсолюти́зм	absolutism
аванга́рд	avant-garde
авиа́ция	aviation
автобиогра́фия	autobiography
атмосфе́ра	atmosphere
бактериоло́гия	bacteriology
балла́да	ballad
баро́метр	barometer
батаре́я	battery
библиогра́фия	bibliography
вака́нсия	vacancy
вандали́зм	vandalism
витами́ны	vitamins
гара́нтия	guarantee
генера́тор	generator
геоло́гия	geology
гладиа́тор	gladiator
дарвини́зм	Darwinism
деклара́ция	declaration
демокра́тия	democracy
диа́гноз	diagnosis
диале́кт	dialect
дие́та	diet
дисципли́на	discipline
жонглёр	juggler

зигза́г	zigzag
игнори́ровать	ignore
иде́я	idea
имита́ция	imitation
индивидуали́зм	individualism
инспе́ктор	inspector
инстру́ктор	instructor
инструме́нт	instrument
калейдоско́п	kaleidoscope
карикату́ра	caricature
компози́тор	composer
коопера́ция	cooperation
корреспонде́нт	correspondent
кри́тика	criticism
лабири́нт	labyrinth
лаборато́рия	laboratory
либерали́зм	liberalism
литерату́ра	literature
маркси́зм	Marxism
медици́на	medicine
мето́дика	method
микроско́п	microscope
негати́в	negative
обсервато́рия	observatory
о́пера	opera
опера́ция	operation
оппози́ция	opposition
оптими́ст	optimist
павильо́н	pavilion
панора́ма	panorama
парази́т	parasite
перспекти́ва	perspective
пикни́к	picnic
пирами́да	pyramid
популя́рный	popular
привиле́гия	privilege

прогре́сс	progress
радиа́тор	radiator
раке́та	rocket
резервуа́р	reservoir
репута́ция	reputation
рефле́ктор	reflector
стати́стика	statistics
та́ктика	tactics
телеско́п	telescope
тео́рия	theory
терминоло́гия	terminology
увертю́ра	overture
университе́т	university
эволю́ция	evolution

B. Geographical Names II

Алжи́р	Algeria
А́встрия	Austria
А́нглия	England
Бе́льгия	Belgium
Брази́лия	Brazil
Гре́ция	Greece
Да́ния	Denmark
Изра́иль	Israel
Ирла́ндия	Ireland
Испа́ния	Spain
Кана́да	Canada
Кита́й	China
Коре́я	Korea
Люксембу́рг	Luxembourg
Маро́кко	Morocco
Нидерла́нды	Netherlands
Но́вая Зела́ндия	New Zealand
Норве́гия	Norway
Португа́лия	Portugal

Та́иланд	Thailand
Ту́рция	Turkey
Швейца́рия	Switzerland
Шве́ция	Sweden
Шотла́ндия	Scotland
Япо́ния	Japan

LESSON 3

A. INTRODUCTION TO THE RUSSIAN ALPHABET

Russian uses the Cyrillic alphabet, which derives from the Greek, whereas English is written with the Latin alphabet. However, there are a few letters that are shared by both languages. Still other letters may be familiar to you from basic mathematics and the names of college fraternities and sororities. As you use this book, you will quickly become familiar with the different letters and sounds, and soon you'll be able to recognize them instantly.

B. THE ALPHABET

Russian	Letter Script		Name
Аа	*A*	*a*	*ah*
Бб	*Б*	*б*	*beh*
Вв	*B*	*в*	*veh*
Гг	*Г*	*г*	*geh*
Дд	*D*	*д*	*deh*
Ее	*E*	*e*	*yeh*
Ёё	*Ё*	*ё*	*yoh*
Жж	*Ж*	*ж*	*zheh*
Зз	*З*	*з*	*zeh*
Ии	*И*	*и*	*ee*
Йй	*Й*	*й*	*ee (i short)*

Кк	*К*	*к*	kah
Лл	*Л*	*л*	ell
Мм	*М*	*м*	em
Нн	*Н*	*н*	en
Оо	*О*	*о*	oh
Пп	*П*	*п*	peh
Рр	*Р*	*р*	err
Сс	*С*	*с*	ess
Тт	*Т*	*т*	teh
Уу	*У*	*у*	ooh
Фф	*Ф*	*ф*	eff
Хх	*Х*	*х*	khah
Цц	*Ц*	*ц*	tseh
Чч	*Ч*	*ч*	cheh
Шш	*Ш*	*ш*	shah
Щщ	*Щ*	*щ*	shchah
Ыы	*Ы*	*ы*	yerih
Ьь	*ь*	*ь*	soft sign
Ъъ	*ъ*	*ъ*	hard sign
Ээ	*Э*	*э*	eh
Юю	*Ю*	*ю*	yuh
Яя	*Я*	*я*	yah

LESSON 4

A. PALATALIZED AND NONPALATALIZED SYLLABLES

Here are all possible combinations of consonants followed by vowels. On the tape, each hard syllable is followed by the palatalized or soft syllable. Listen carefully and try to hear the difference. Imitate. Listen again. Try to hear the difference in your own pronunciation.

ба ва га да жа за ка ла ма на па ра са та фа ха ца ча ша ща

бя вя гя дя зя кя ля мя ня пя ря ся тя фя

бо во го до жо зо ко ло мо но по ро со то фо хо цо чо шо що

бё вё гё дё жё зё кё лё мё нё пё рё сё тё фё чё шё щё

бу ву гу ду жу зу ку лу му ну пу ру су ту фу ху цу чу шу щу

бю вю дю жю* зю кю лю мю ню пю рю сю тю фю хю

бэ вэ гэ дэ зэ кэ лэ мэ нэ пэ рэ сэ тэ фэ хэ цэ

бе ве ге де же зе ке ле ме не пе ре се те фе хе це че ше ще

* Pronounced soft (palatalized), as in жюри (jury), a word of foreign origin.

бы вы ды зы лы мы ны пы ры сы ты фы хы цы

би ви ги ди жи зи ки ли ми ни пи ри си ти фи хи ци чи ши щи

NOTICE

Keep in mind the following points:

жо and жё }	are pronounced alike.
цэ and це	
цы and ц }	the letters ж, ц, ш
шо and шё	are always hard.
чо and чё }	the letters ч and щ are
що and щё	always soft.

LESSON 5

A. VOWELS

1. The letter A
   a. When stressed, it is pronounced like the English *ah*:

а́рмия	army
ла́мпа	lamp
ма́ло	little

   b. When unstressed, before a stressed syllable, it is pronounced *ah*, but shorter.

   c. In most other positions it is given a neuter sound–i.e., like that of the letter *a* in *sofa*:

каранда́ш	pencil
магази́н	store
аванга́рд	avant-garde

2. The letter О
   a. When stressed, it is pronounced *aw*, as in
      law:

он	he
до́брый	pleasant

   b. When unstressed, it is either in first place
      before the stressed syllable or used initially
      and is pronounced *ah*:

Бори́с	Boris
она́	she
оно́	it
отвеча́ть	to answer

   c. In all other positions it is given a neuter
      sound–i.e., like the *a* in *sofa*.

хорошо́	well
пло́хо	badly
молоко́	milk

3. The letter У
   is pronounced both stressed and
   unstressed like the English *ooh*:

стул	chair
суп	soup
у́тро	morning
туда́	there (in that direction)
уро́к	lesson
узнава́ть	to find out
учи́тель	teacher

4. The letter Ы

is always pronounced like the short vowel sound
created between the letters *b* and *l* in *table*:

ты	you
мы	we
вы	you *(pl.)*
мы́ло	soap
малы̀	small (predicative form)
столы́	tables
была́	she was

5. The letter Э

is pronounced like the *eh* in *echo*:

э́то	this
э́ти	these
поэ́т	poet
эта́п	stage

NOTICE

The function of the following vowels—е, ё, и, ю, я—which are
preceded by a glide (the sound similar to the final sound in the
English word *may*) is the palatalization of the preceding consonant, to which they lose the above-mentioned glide. However,
when they follow a vowel or soft or hard signs, or when they
appear initially, they are pronounced as in the alphabet—i.e., with
an initial glide.

6. The letter И

always palatalizes the preceding consonant and
is pronounced like the *ee* in *beet* except after the
letters **ж, ц, ш,** which are never palatalized;
then **и** is pronounced like the Russian sound **ы**:

си́ла	strength
Ли́за	Liza

мой	my
твой	your
никогда́	never
иногда́	sometimes
ши́на[1]	tire
жить[1]	live

7. The letter Й

a. It is never stressed. It is pronounced like the final sound in the English word *boy*:

мой	my
пойти́	to go
споко́йно	quietly

b. It is very seldom used initially, except in some words of foreign origin:

Нью-Йорк	New York

8. The letter Е

a. It always palatalizes the preceding consonant, except the letters ж, ц, ш. When stressed, it is pronounced like the *eh* in *echo*, losing its glide to the palatalization of the preceding consonant:

нет	no, not
Ве́ра	Vera, faith
сесть	to sit down

b. In unstressed positions it is pronounced like the *ee* in *beet*:

всегда́	always

[1] Here и is pronounced ы because ж and щ are never palatalized.

| сестра́ | sister |
| жена́* | wife |

c. Initially, or after another vowel, it is pronounced with the glide—stressed, like *yeh*, or unstressed, like *yeeh*:

ей	to her
её	her
пое́здка	trip

9. The letter Ё
   always palatalizes the preceding consonant and is always stressed. In the middle of the word it is pronounced *aw*. Initially, or after another vowel, it retains its glide and is pronounced *yaw*:

мёд	honey
тётя	aunt
ёлка	fir tree
моё	my (*n*)
ещё	yet, still

10. The letter Я
    a. It always palatalizes the preceding consonant. When stressed in the middle of the word, it is pronounced *ah;* when unstressed, it is pronounced like the neuter sound *a* in *sofa*.

мя́со	meat
мая́к	lighthouse
тётя	aunt

* Unstressed е is pronounced и, but и after ж is pronounced ы; hence, here е is pronounced ы.

b. When used initially, it retains its glide; when stressed, it is pronounced *yah;* when unstressed, *yee*:

я́блоко	apple
январь	January
язы́к	language, tongue

11. The letter Ю
a. It always palatalizes the preceding consonant. It is pronounced *ooh* in the body of the word:

Лю́ба	Lyuba
люблю́	I love
люби́ть	to love

b. When used initially, it retains its glide and is pronounced yooh:

| ю́бка | skirt |
| юбиле́й | jubilee |

12. The letter Ь
is called the "soft" sign; it palatalizes the preceding consonant, allowing the following vowel to retain its glide:

пье́са	play
пья́ный	drunk
свинья́	pig

13. The letter Ъ
is called the "hard" sign. It indicates that the preceding consonant remains hard and that the following vowel retains its glide.

| объём | volume |
| объясня́ть | explain |

LESSON 6

A. CONSONANTS

Russian consonants, like those in every language, may be voiced or voiceless. The distinction between voiced and voiceless consonants is based on one aspect of otherwise identical articulation: in voiced consonants vocal cords are involved in articulation, while in voiceless consonants they are not. The pairs are:

б в г д ж з	(voiced)	b v g d j z
п ф к т ш с	(voiceless)	p f k t sh s

When two consonants are pronounced together, both must be either voiced or voiceless. In Russian, the second one always remains as it is and the first one changes accordingly.

всё, все, вчера	**В**=v, pronounced *f*
сделать, сдать	**С**=s, pronounced *z*

The preposition в (in) is very often pronounced *f*. в школе (in school) is pronounced *fshkaw-lee*.

Russian consonants can also be soft or hard, i.e., palatalized or nonpalatalized, when followed by the letters е, ё, и, ю, я or ь; exceptions are the consonants ж, ш, ц, which are always hard.

This looks complicated, but it is much easier to learn this in the beginning and to begin speaking correctly, than it is to try to correct erroneous pronunciation later on. Listen carefully and try to hear the above-mentioned differences.

Б

1. Pronounced like the *b* in *bread*:

брат	brother
бума́га	paper
бага́ж	baggage

2. Palatalized:

бе́лый	white
бино́кль	binoculars

3. Voiceless, like the *p* at the end of a word or before a voiceless consonant:

ю́бка	skirt
зуб	tooth
хлеб	bread

4. Voiceless palatalized:

дробь	buckshot
зыбь	ripple

В

1. Pronounced like the *v* in *very*:

ваш	your
вот	here
вода́	water

2. Palatalized:

вéра	faith
конвéрт	envelope
весь	all

3. Voiceless, like the *f* at the end of a word or before a voiceless consonant:

Кѝев	Kiev
в шкóле	in school
вчерá	yesterday
кров	shelter

4. Voiceless palatalized:

кровь	blood

Г

1. Pronounced like the *g* in *good*:

газéта	newspaper
гдe	where
гармóния	harmony

2. Palatalized:

гитáра	guitar
геомéтрия	geometry

3. Like the Russian **x** before **к**:

легкó	lightly, easily
мягко	softly

4. Like the *v* in the genitive ending, masculine and neuter:

его́	his
ничего́	nothing
сего́дня	today

5. Voiceless, like the *k* at the end of a word:

рог	horn
четве́рг	Thursday

Д

1. Pronounced like the *d* in *door*:

дом	house
родно́й	kindred

2. Palatalized:

де́рево	wood
оди́н	one

3. Voiceless, like the *t* at the end of a word or before a voiceless consonant:

обе́д	dinner
подко́ва	horseshoe
по́дпись	signature

4. Voiceless palatalized:

грудь	breast

Ж

1. Pronounced like the *s* in *measure*: always hard:

жар	heat
жена́	wife
жить	to live
пожа́р	fire

2. Voiceless, like the *sh* at the end of a word or before a voiceless consonant:

ло́жка	spoon
муж	husband

З

1. Pronounced like the *z* in *zebra*:

зда́ние	building
знать	to know

2. Palatalized:

зелёный	green
зима́	winter

3. Voiceless, like the *s* at the end of a word or before a voiceless consonant:

ползти́	crawl
воз	cart

К

1. Pronounced like the *k* in *kept*:

кни́га	book
класс	class
каранда́ш	pencil

2. Palatalized:

ке́пка	cap
кероси́н	kerosene
Ки́ев	Kiev
кино́	movie

3. Voiced, like the *g* in *good*, before a voiced consonant:

вокза́л	railroad station
экза́мен	examination
к бра́ту	to the brother

Л

1. Pronounced like the *l* in *look*:

ло́жка	spoon
ла́мпа	lamp
мел	chalk

2. Palatalized:

любо́вь	love
лёгкий	light
мель	shallow place
боль	pain

LESSON 7

A. CONSONANTS II

М

1. Pronounced like the *m* in *man*:

ма́ма	mama
магни́т	magnet
дом	house
паро́м	ferry

2. Palatalized:

мя́со	meat
ми́на	mine

Н

1. Pronounced like the *n* in *noon*:

нос	nose
нож	knife
балко́н	balcony

2. Palatalized:

не́бо	sky
неде́ля	week
ня́ня	nurse
ко́нь	horse

П

1. Palatalized:

пе́рвый	first
письмо́	letter
цепь	chain

Р

1. Pronounced like the *r* in *root*:

ру́сский	Russian
пара́д	parade
пода́рок	gift
рука́	hand

2. Palatalized:

рис	rice
поря́док	order
дверь	door

С

1. Pronounced like the *s* in *see*:

сон	dream
суп	soup
свет	light
мя́со	meat
ма́сло	butter

2. Palatalized:

се́вер	north
село́	village
весь	all

3. Voiced, like the *z* before a voiced consonant:

сде́лать	to do
сгоре́ть	to burn down

Т

1. Pronounced like the *t* in *table*:

таба́к	tobacco
тот	that
стол	table
тогда́	then

2. Palatalized:

тень	shade
стена́	wall

3. Voiced like the *d* before a voiced consonant:

отда́ть	to give away
отгада́ть	to guess

Ф

1. Pronounced like the *f* in *friend*:

фа́брика	factory
Фра́нция	France
фарфо́р	porcelain

2. Palatalized:

афи́ша	poster

3. Voiced, like the *v* before a voiced consonant:

афга́нец	Afghan

X

1. Pronounced like the *h* in *hat*, but much softer:

ти́хо	quietly
хорошо́	well
те́хника	technique
блоха́	flea

2. Palatalized

хи́на	quinine
хи́мия	chemistry

Ц

Pronounced like the *ts* in *gets;* always hard:

цвето́к	flower
цепь	chain
цирк	circus
пацие́нт	patient (n.)
пе́рец	pepper

Ч

1. Pronounced like the *ch* in *church;* always soft:

чай	tea
час	hour
ча́сто	often
чемода́н	suitcase

2. Sometimes pronounced like the *sh* in *shall*:

| что | what |
| конéчно | of course |

Ш

Pronounced like the *sh* in *shall;* always hard:

шаг за шáгом	step after step
шáхматы	chess
шúна	tire
шёлк	silk
шерсть	wool
ты говорúшь	you speak *(sing.)*

Щ

Pronounced like the *shch* in the word combination *fresh cheese;* always soft:

щека	cheek
щётка	brush
пóмощь	help
посещéние	visit

This completes the rules for pronunciation and reading. Read these rules over and over again. Listen to the tapes over and over again. You have learned them not when you have read and understood the rules, but when you can remember and repeat the sounds and words correctly without looking at the book. Master these, and you will speak Russian well.

1. Remember which syllable is stressed.
2. Remember that unstressed o is pronounced
    ah in prestressed position.
3. Remember that when two consonants are next
    to each other, the first changes according to the
    second.
4. Remember that unstressed e is pronounced
    ee.
5. Remember that the letters е, ё, и, ю, я, and
    ь palatalize the preceding consonant.

LESSON 8

A. MASCULINE, FEMININE, NEUTER, PLURAL

All Russian nouns, pronouns, adjectives, and ordinal numbers, as well as some cardinal numbers and
even several verb forms, have gender: masculine, feminine, or neuter. In the plural there is only one form for
all genders.

1. Most nouns, pronouns, and past tense forms of
   verbs end on:

MASCULINE	FEMININE	NEUTER	PLURAL
hard consonant	а, я	о, е	а, ы, и

2. Most adjectives, ordinal numbers, and participles
   end on:

MASCULINE	FEMININE	NEUTER	PLURAL
ой, ый, ий	ая, яя	ое, ее	ые, ие
он	она	оно́	они́
he	she	it	they
мой	моя́	моё	мои́
my	my	my	my
мой брат	моя́ сестра́	моё окно́	мои́ де́ти
my brother	my sister	my window	my children
твой	твоя́	твоё	твои́
your (sing.)	your	your	our (fam.)
твой	твоя́	твоё	твои́
каранда́ш	кни́га	пальто́	де́ньги
your pencil	your book	your coat	your money
наш дом	на́ша	на́ше	на́ши
	кварти́ра	село́	кни́ги
our house	our apartment	our village	our books
ваш	ва́ша	ва́ше	ва́ши
your (pl., polite)	your	your	your
ваш стул	ва́ша ла́мпа	ва́ше по́ле	ва́ши руба́шки
your chair	your lamp	your field	your shirts
э́тот	э́та	э́то	э́ти
this	this	this	these
бе́лый	бе́лая	бе́лое	бе́лые
white	white	white	white
Э́тот стол	Э́та стена́	Э́то пла́тье	Э́ти сте́ны
бе́лый.	бе́лая.	бе́лое.	бе́лые.
This table is white.	This wall is white.	This dress is white.	These walls are white.
большо́й	больша́я	большо́е	больши́е
large	large	large	large
его́	её	его́	их
his	her	its	their
его́ оте́ц	её оте́ц		их оте́ц
his father	her father		their father
чей оте́ц	чья мать	чьё окно́	чьи кни́ги
whose father	whose mother	whose window	whose books

свой	своя́	своё	свои́
one's own	one's own	one's own	one's own
кра́сный	кра́сная	кра́сное	кра́сные
red	red	red	red
чёрный	чёрная	чёрное	чёрные
black	black	black	black
си́ний	си́няя	си́нее	си́ние
blue	blue	blue	blue
оди́н	одна́	одно́	одни́
one	one	one	alone, only
два	две	два	
two	two	two	
пе́рвый	пе́рвая	пе́рвое	пе́рвые
first	first	first	first
второ́й	втора́я	второ́е	вторы́е
second	second	second	second
тре́тий	тре́тья	тре́тье	тре́тьи
third	third	third	third

NOTICE

Pronouns, adjectives, and ordinal numbers always agree in gender with the nouns they modify.

QUIZ 1

Match the letters with the numbers of the correct translations.

1. оди́н	a.	this (m.)
2. кра́сная	b.	my children
3. де́ньги	c.	This wall is white
4. он	d.	our books
5. ва́ша ла́мпа	e.	her
6. э́та стена́ бе́лая	f.	he
7. э́тот	g.	first (f.)
8. на́ши кни́ги	h.	red (f.)
9. мои́ де́ти	i.	children
10. мой брат	j.	one (m.)
11. её	k.	these
12. де́ти	l.	money

13. пе́рвая		m.	your field
14. ва́ше по́ле		n.	your lamp
15. э́ти		o.	my sister
16. моя́ сестра́		p.	my brother

ANSWERS
1–j; 2–h; 3–l; 4–f; 5–n; 6–c; 7–a; 8–d; 9–b; 10–p; 11–e; 12–i;
13–g; 14–m; 15–k; 16–o.

LESSON 9

A. CHARACTERISTICS OF THE CASES

With few exceptions, all nouns, pronouns, and
adjectives decline. Each declension has six cases
used to answer the following question words in
their respective case forms (some preceded by the
appropriate prepositions):

Case	Questions
Nominative (subject):	**Кто? Что?** Who? What?
Genitive (possession, negation):	**Кого́? Чего́?** Whom? What? **От кого́? От чего́?** From whom? From what? **У кого́? У чего́?** At/by whom (what)? **Без кого́? Без чего́?** Without whom (what)?
Dative (indirect object):	**Кому́? Чему́?** To whom? To what? **К кому́? К чему́?** To whom? To what (direction towards)?

Accusative (direct object):	**Кого? Что?**
	Whom? What?
	Куда?
	Where (direction towards)?
Instrumental (object as an instrument, manner of action):	**Кем? Чем?**
	By whom? By what?
	С кем? С чем?
	With whom? With what?
Prepositional or Locative (location, also with certain prepositions):	**О ком? О чём?**
	About whom? about what?
	В ком? В чём?
	In whom? In what?
	Где?
	Where?

1. The nominative case supplies the subject of the sentence.

2. The genitive is the case of possession and is also used with many prepositions, the most common of which are без (without), для (for), до (up to), из (out of), около (near, by, about), от (from), после (after), у (at or by).

3. The dative case is used in the meaning of "to whom." Prepositions governing the dative case are к (to) and по (along).

4. The accusative is the direct-object case. Prepositions used with this case include в (to, into), за (behind), на (to, into, on) in the sense of direction.

5. The instrumental case indicates the manner of action or the instrument with which the action is performed. Prepositions governing the instrumental case include между (between), перед (in front of), and с (with).

6. The prepositional or locative case indicates location but is also used when speaking about something or someone. The prepositions most frequently used with this case are в (in), на (on), о (about), and при (in the presence of).

B. Word Study

звони́ть-позвони́ть	to call (on the phone)
почему́	why
вме́сте	together
потому́ что	because
говори́ть-сказа́ть	to say
уже́	already
непра́вильно	incorrectly
ка́ждый	each, every one
зада́ча	problem, task

LESSON 10

A. Кто (Who?) and Никто/Некто (No One/Someone)

NOTICE

When used with prepositions, the negative expressions никто́/не́кто split into three words: the negative particle ни/не, the preposition, and the declined form of кто. (Никто́ is used only with negated verbs, не́кто only with non-negated verbs, primarily in impersonal sentences). This will be clear after you study these phrases.

Nominative:

Кто он?	Who is he?
Кто она́?	Who is she?

Кто они́?	Who are they?
Кто э́то сде́лал?	Who did this?
Кто сказа́л э́то?	Who said this?

Negative:

Никто́ не сде́лал.	No one did his.
Никто́ не сказа́л.	No one said it.
Не́кто был здесь.	Someone was here.

Genitive:

Кого́ нет до́ма?	Who is not at home?
У кого́ он живёт?	At whose place (by whom) does he live?
Для кого́ э́то?	For whom is that?

Negative:

Никого́ нет до́ма.	No one is at home.
Э́то ни для кого́.	This is for no one.
Не́ у кого жить.	There is no one to live with (at).

Dative:

Кому́ вы э́то сказа́ли?	To whom did you say that?
Кому́ вы да́ли мою́ кни́гу?	To whom did you give my book?
К кому́ вы идёте?	To whom are you going?
Кому́ здесь хо́лодно?	Who is cold here? (To whom is it cold?)

Negative:

Не говори́те никому́.	Don't tell anyone.
Не́кому написа́ть.	There's no one to write to.

Accusative:

Кого́ вы зна́ете здесь?	Whom do you know here?

На кого́ она́ похо́жа?	Whom does she look like?

Negative:

Я здесь никого́ не зна́ю.	I don't know anyone here.
Не́ на кого положи́ться.	Nobody to rely on.

Instrumental:

С кем вы бы́ли в теа́тре вчера́?	With whom were you at the theater yesterday?
Ке́м вы хоти́те быть?	What do you want to be?

Negative:

Я ни с ке́м не́ был в теа́тре.	I was with no one at the theater.
Не́ с кем поговори́ть.	Nobody to talk to.

Locative/Prepositional:

О ко́м вы говори́те?	Whom are you talking about?
На ко́м он жена́т?	To whom is he married?

Negative:

Мы ни о ко́м не говори́м.	We are not talking about anyone.
Он ни на ко́м не жена́т.	He is not married to anyone.

QUIZ 2

Fill in the blanks with the proper form of кто.

1. _____ сказа́л э́то?	Who said it?
2. _____ нет до́ма?	Who isn't at home?

3. _____ здесь хо́лодно?	Who is cold here?
4. _____ вы да́ли мою кни́гу?	To whom did you give my book?
5. _____ вы хоти́те быть?	Whom do you want to be?
6. На _____ он жена́т?	To whom is he married?
7. Не с _____ говори́ть.	No one to talk with.
8. _____ вы зна́ете здесь?	Whom do you know here?
9. Я _____ здесь не зна́ю.	I don't know anyone here.
10. О _____ вы говори́те?	Whom are you talking about?

ANSWERS

1. кто 2. кого́ 3. кому́; 4. кому́ 5. кем 6. ком 7. кем
8. кого́ 9. никого́ 10. ком.

B. Что? (WHAT?) AND Ничего/Нечего (NOTHING)

NOTICE

As with никто́/не́кто, when used with prepositions, the negative expressions ничего́/не́чего split into three words: the particle ни/не, the preposition, and the declined form of что (чего́ in ничего́/не́чего is the genitive form of что).

Nominative:

Что́ э́то?	What is it?
Что́ там?	What is there?
Я не зна́ю, что э́то.	I don't know what it is.
Что́ э́то тако́е?	What is this?
Что́ э́то за зда́ние?	What kind of a building is this?
Что но́вого?	What's new?
Что зна́чит э́то сло́во?	What does this word mean?
Что он сказа́л?	What did he say?

Set expression:

Ни за что́ на све́те!	Not for anything in the world!

Genitive:

Для чего́ э́то?	What's this for?
Чего́ то́лько нет в э́том магази́не!	What they don't have in this store!
От чего́ у меня́ боли́т голова́?	Why [what from] does my head ache?

Negative:

Он ничего́ не сказа́л.	He didn't say anything.
Не́ на что жить.	Nothing to live on.
В э́том магази́не ничего́ нет.	There is nothing in this store.
Не́чего беспоко́иться.	Nothing to worry (about).

Set expression:

Посмотри́те, до чего́ э́то дошло́.	Look what it has come to.
Чего́ он то́лько не ви́дел!	What hasn't he seen!

Dative:

Чему́ вы удивля́етесь!	What are you surprised at!
К чему́ всё э́то?	What's all this for?

Negative:

Э́то ни к чему́.	This is unnecessary [for nothing].
Не́чему удивля́ться.	Nothing to be surprised at.

Set expression:

Чему́ быть–тому́ не минова́ть.	What's to be, will be.

Accusative:

Что́ вы хоти́те посмотре́ть?	What would you like to see?

Negative:
    Не на что жить.   Nothing to live on.

Instrumental:
    Чем вы пишете?   What are you writing with?

    Зачем вы пришли?   Why [what for] did you come?

Negative:
    Она меня ничем не может удивить.   She cannot surprise me with anything.

Locative/Prepositional:
    О чём вы говорите?   What are you talking about?

    При чём тут я?   What do I have to do with it?

Negative:
    Я ни о чём не говорю.   I am not talking about anything.

    Не о чем сейчас писать.   There is nothing to write about now.

Set expression:
    В чём дело?   What's the matter?

C. DECLENSIONS OF NOUNS, ADJECTIVES, AND PRONOUNS

Here are the basic forms of declensions of nouns, adjectives, and pronouns.

Do not try to learn these forms. It is better to remember sentences as you continue with the tapes. As you learn sentences, you can refer to these tables to find out to which group the new words belong.

Grammar is a description of a language, not a set

of rules by which a language should abide. Grammar describes many different groups in the language and many exceptions to these groups. The more groups and the more exceptions there are, the richer the language.

1. Nouns

Masculine Singular

	HARD		SOFT	
	Animate	Inanimate	Animate	Inanimate
	student	question	inhabitant	shed
Nom.	студе́нт	вопро́с	жи́тел-ь	сара́-й
Gen.	студе́нт-а	вопро́с-а	жи́тел-я	сара́-я
Dat.	студе́нт-у	вопро́с-у	жи́тел-ю	сара́-ю
Acc.	студе́нт-а	вопро́с	жи́тел-я	сара́-й
Inst.	студе́нт-ом	вопро́с-ом	жи́тел-ем	сара́-ем
Prep.	о студе́нт-е	о вопро́с-е	о жи́тел-е	о сара́-е

Masculine Plural

Nom.	студе́нт-ы	вопро́с-ы	жи́тел-и	сара́-и
Gen.	студе́нт-ов	вопро́с-ов	жи́тел-ей	сара́-ев
Dat.	студе́нт-ам	вопро́с-ам	жи́тел-ям	сара́-ям
Acc.	студе́нт-ов	вопро́с-ы	жи́тел-ей	сара́-и
Inst.	студе́нт-ами	вопро́с-ами	жи́тел-ями	сара́-ями
Prep.	о студе́нт-ах	о вопро́с-ах	о жи́тел-ях	о сара́-ях

NOTICE

The accusative case of animate masculine nouns is the same as the genitive, and of inanimate masculine nouns is the same as the nominative.

FEMININE SINGULAR

	HARD		SOFT
	room	earth	family
Nom.	ко́мнат-а	земля́	семья́
Gen.	ко́мнат-ы	земл-и́	семь-и́
Dat.	ко́мнат-е	земл-е́	семь-е́
Acc.	ко́мнат-у	зе́мл-ю	семь-ю́
Inst.	ко́мнат-ой(ою)	земл-ёй	семь-ёй
Prep.	о ко́мнат-е	о земл-е́	о семь-е́

FEMININE PLURAL

	HARD		SOFT
Nom.	ко́мнат-ы	зе́мл-и	се́мь-и
Gen.	ко́мнат	земе́л-ь	сем-е́й
Dat.	ко́мнат-ам	зе́мл-ям	се́мь-ям
Acc.	ко́мнат-ы	зе́мл-и	се́мь-и
Inst.	ко́мнат-ами	зе́мл-ями	се́мь-ями
Prep.	о ко́мнат-ах	о зе́мл-ях	о се́мь-ях

NEUTER SINGULAR

	HARD		SOFT
	window	sea	wish
Nom.	окно́	мо́ре	жела́ние
Gen.	окн-а́	мо́р-я	жела́н-ия
Dat.	окн-у́	мо́р-ю	жела́н-ию
Acc.	окн-о́	мо́р-е	жела́н-ие
Inst.	окн-о́м	мо́р-ем	жела́н-ием
Prep.	об[1] окн-е́	о мо́р-е	о жела́нии

NEUTER PLURAL

	HARD		SOFT
Nom.	о́кн-а	мор-я́	жела́н-ия
Gen.	ок-о́н	мор-е́й	жела́н-ий
Dat.	о́кн-ам	мор-я́м	жела́н-иям
Acc.	о́кн-а	мор-я́	жела́н-ия
Inst.	о́кн-ами	мор-я́ми	жела́н-иями
Prep.	об[1] о́кн-ах	о мор-я́х	о жела́н-иях

[1] б is added to the preposition here for the sake of euphony.

2. SOME IRREGULAR DECLENSIONS

	MASC.	FEM.	NEUT.	
		SINGULAR		
	road	mother	name	child
Nom.	путь	мать	и́мя	дитя́
Gen.	пут-и́	ма́т-ери	и́м-ени	дит-я́ти[1]
Dat.	пут-и́	ма́т-ери	и́м-ени	дит-я́ти[1]
Acc.	путь	мать	и́мя	дитя́
Inst.	пут-ём	ма́т-ерью	и́м-енем	дитя́тей[1]
Prep.	о пут-и́	о ма́т-ери	об и́м-ени	о дит-я́ти[1]

		PLURAL		
Nom	пут-и́	ма́т-ери	име-на́	де́т-и
Gen.	пут-е́й	мат-ере́й	им-ён	дет-е́й
Dat.	пут-я́м	мат-еря́м	им-ена́м	де́т-ям
Acc.	пут-и́	мат-ере́й	им-ена́	дет-е́й[2]
Inst.	пут-я́ми	мат-еря́ми	им-ена́ми	дет-ьми́
Prep.	о пут-я́х	о мат-еря́х	об им-ена́х	о де́т-ях

3. ADJECTIVES

		SINGULAR	
	MASC.	FEM.	NEUT.
	ый	ая	ое
Nom.	но́вый=new	но́вая	но́вое
Gen.	но́в-ого	но́в-ой	но́в-ого
Dat.	но́в-ому	но́в-ой	но́в-ому
Acc.	same as nom. or gen.	но́в-ую	но́в-ое
Inst.	но́в-ым	но́в-ой	но́в-ым
Prep.	о но́в-ом	о но́в-ой	о но́вом

---

[1] Old form seldom used.

[2] The accusative case of animate neuter nouns is the same as the genitive.

	ой	ая	ое
	ой	ая	ое
Nom.	дорогóй=dear	дорогáя	дорогóе
Gen.	дорог-óго	дорог-óй	дорог-óго
Dat.	дорог-óму	дорог-óй	дорог-óму
Acc.	same as nom. or gen.	дорог-ýю	дорог-óе
Inst.	дорог-и́м	дорог-ой	дорог-и́м
Prep.	о дорог-óм	о дорог-óй	о дорог-óм

PLURAL

ALL GENDERS

Nom.	нóв-ые	дорог-и́е
Gen.	нóв-ых	дорог-и́х
Dat.	нóв-ым	дорог-и́м
Acc.	same as nom. or gen.	same as nom. or gen.
Inst.	нóв-ыми	дорог-и́ми
rep.	о нóв-ых	о дорог-и́х

	SINGULAR			PLURAL
	MASC.	FEM.	NEUT.	ALL GENDERS
	ий	яя	ee	ие
Nom.	си́н-ий blue	си́н-яя	си́н-ее	си́н-ие
Gen.	си́н-его	си́н-ей	си́н-его	си́н-их
Dat.	си́н-ему	си́н-ей	си́н-ему	си́н-им
Acc.	same as nom.or gen	си́н-юю	си́н-ее	same as nom.or gen.
Inst.	си́н-им	си́н-ей	си́н-им	си́н-ими
Prep.	о си́н-ем	о си́н-ей	о си́н-ем	о си́н-их

4. Pronouns

	SINGUL.	PLUR.	SINGUL.	PLURAL AND POLITE	SINGULAR OR PLURAL
	I	we	you	you	-self
Nom.	я	мы	ты	вы	–
Gen.	меня́	нас	тебя́	вас	себя́
Dat.	мне́	нам	тебе́	вам	себе́
Acc.	меня́	нас	тебя́	вас	себя́
Inst.	мно́ю(ой)	на́ми	тобо́й	ва́ми	собо́ю(ой)
Prep.	обо мне́	о нас	о тебе́	о вас	о себе́

	SINGULAR			PLURAL (ALL GENDERS)
	he	she	it	they
Nom.	он	она́	оно́	они́
Gen.	его́	её	его́	их
Dat.	ему́	ей	ему́	им
Acc.	его́	её	его́	их
Inst.	им	ею	им	и́ми
Prep.	о нём	о ней	о нём	о них

	SINGULAR my			PLURAL my ALL GENDERS
	MASC.	FEM.	NEUTER	
Nom.	мой	моя́	моё	мои́
Gen.	моего́	мое́й	моего́	мои́х
Dat.	моему́	мое́й	моему́	мои́м
Acc.	same as nom. or gen.	мою́	same as nom. or gen.	same as nom. or gen.
Inst.	мои́м	мое́й	мои́м	мои́ми
Prep.	моём	о мое́й	моём	о мои́х

NOTICE

Твой (your, *sing.*), свой (one's own, their own) are declined in the same way.

In expressing the possessive in the third person, the genetive case of the pronouns он, она́, оно, они–его́ (his), её (hers), его́ (its), их (theirs)–is used. These pronouns always agree with the gender and number of the possessor.

Их дом хоро́ший.	Their house is nice.
Я ви́дела их дочь.	I saw their daughter.
Он взял её кни́ги.	He took her books.
Его́ кни́га бо́лее интере́сная.	His book is more interesting.

	SINGULAR our			PLURAL our
	MASC.	FEM.	NEUTER	ALL GENDERS
Nom.	наш	на́ша	на́ше	на́ши
Gen.	наш-его	на́ш-ей	на́ш-его	на́ш-их
Dat.	на́ш-ему	на́ш-ей	на́ш-ему	на́ш-им
Acc.	same as nom. or gen.	на́ш-у	same as nom. or gen.	same as nom. or gen.
Inst.	на́ш-им	на́ш-ей	на́ш-им	на́ш-ими
Prep.	о на́ш-ем	о на́ш-ей	о на́ш-ем	о на́ш-их

NOTICE

Ваш (your, *pl. or polite*) is declined in the same way.

	SINGULAR all			PLURAL all
	MASC.	FEM.	NEUTER	ALL GENDERS
Nom.	весь	вся	всё	все
Gen.	вс-его́	вс-ей	вс-его́	вс-ех
Dat.	все-му́	вс-ей	вс-ему́	вс-ем
Acc.	same as nom. or gen.	вс-ю	всё	same as nom. or gen.
Inst.	вс-ем	вс-ей	вс-ем	вс-е́ми
Prep.	обо вс-ём	обо вс-ей	обо вс-ём	обо вс-ех

| | SINGULAR this | | | PLURAL these |
	MASC.	FEM.	NEUTER	ALL GENDERS
Nom.	э́тот	э́та	э́то	э́ти
Gen.	э́т-ого	э́т-ой	э́т-ого	э́т-их
Dat.	э́т-ому	э́т-ой	э́т-ому	э́т-им
Acc.	same as nom. or gen.	э́т-у	э́то	same as nom. or gen.
Inst.	э́т-им	э́т-ой	э́т-им	э́т-ими
Prep.	об э́т-ом	об э́т-ой	об э́т-ом	об э́т-их

| | SINGULAR that | | | PLURAL those |
	MASC.	FEM.	NEUTER	ALL GENDERS
Nom.	тот	та	то	те
Gen.	т-ого́	т-ой	т-ого́	т-ех
Dat.	т-ому́	т-ой	т-ому́	т-ем
Acc.	same as nom. or gen.	т-у	т-о	same as nom. or gen.
Inst.	т-ем	т-ой	т-ем	т-е́ми
Prep.	о т-ом	о т-ой	о т-ом	о т-ех

| | SINGULAR oneself | | | PLURAL themselves |
	MASC.	FEM.	NEUTER	ALL GENDERS
Nom.	сам	сама́	само́	са́ми
Gen.	сам-ого́	сам-о́й	сам-ого́	сам-и́х
Dat.	сам-ому́	сам-о́й	сам-ому́	сам-и́м
Acc.	сам-ого́	сам-оё	сам-о́	сам-и́х
Inst.	сам-и́м	сам-о́й	сам-и́м	сам-и́ми
Prep.	о сам-о́м	о сам-о́й	о сам-о́м	о сам-и́х

QUIZ 3

Fill in the blanks with the proper form of **что**.

1. Я не зна́ю, _____ э́то. I don't know what it is.
2. _____ но́вого? What's new?
3. _____ вы пи́шете? What are you writing?

4. Для _____ э́то?   What's this for?
5. К _____ всё э́то?   What's all this for?
6. _____ быть—того́ не минова́ть.   What's to be, will be.
7. _____ вы удивля́етесь?   What are you surprised at?
8. О _____ вы говори́те?   What are you talking about?
9. В _____ де́ло?   What's the matter?
10. _____ вы пи́шете?   What are you writing with?

ANSWERS
1. что 2. что 3 что 4. чего́ 5. чему́ 6. чему́ 7. чему́ 8. чём
9. чём 10. чем.

LESSON 11

A. NUMBERS

оди́н	one
два	two
три	three
четы́ре	four
пять	five
шесть	six
семь	seven
во́семь	eight
де́вять	nine
де́сять	ten

B. DAYS AND MONTHS [1]

понеде́льник	Monday
вто́рник	Tuesday
среда́	Wednesday
четве́рг	Thursday
пя́тница	Friday
суббо́та	Saturday
воскресе́нье	Sunday

[1] Neither the names of the days nor of the months are capitalized.

янва́рь	January
февра́ль	February
март	March
апре́ль	April
май	May
ию́нь	June
ию́ль	July
а́вгуст	August
сентя́брь	September
октя́брь	October
ноя́брь	November
дека́брь	December

C. Seasons and Directions

весна́	spring
весно́й	in the spring
ле́то	summer
ле́том	in the summer
о́сень	autumn
о́сенью	in the autumn
зима́	winter
зимо́й	in the winter
се́вер	north
юг	south
восто́к	east
за́пад	west

D. Word Study

профе́ссия	profession
ма́льчик	boy
де́вочка	girl
пока́зывать-показа́ть	to show
свобо́дный	free
повторя́ть-повтори́ть	to repeat

иногда́	sometimes
наро́д	the people
ме́дленно	slowly

LESSON 12

A. GREETINGS

у́тро	morning
у́тром	in the morning
день	day
днём	during the day (afternoon)
ве́чер	evening
ве́чером	in the evening
ночь	night
но́чью	during the night
сего́дня	today
вчера́	yesterday
за́втра	tomorrow
до́брое	good
у́тро	morning
До́брое у́тро.	Good morning.
до́брое	good
день	day/afternoon
До́брый день.	Good day. Good afternoon.
ве́чер	evening
До́брый ве́чер.	Good evening.
как	how
дела́	things
Как дела́?	How are things?
как	how
вы	you
себя́	yourself
чу́вствуете	feel

Как вы себя чу́вствуете?	How are you feeling?
спаси́бо	thank you
хорошо́	well
Спаси́бо, хорошо́.	Well, thank you.
ничего́	nothing
Спаси́бо, ничего́.	Thank you, not bad.
нельзя́	impossible [one may not]
лу́чше	better
Как нельзя́ лу́чше.	Couldn't be any better.
А вы?	And you?
То́же хорошо́, спаси́бо.	Also well, thank you.
Прекра́сно.	Excellent.
Что но́вого?	What's new?
Всё по-ста́рому.	Everything's the same [all as of old].

B. Last Month, Last Year, etc.

послеза́втра	day after tomorrow
че́рез два дня	in two days
че́рез пять дней	in five days
че́рез ме́сяц	in a month
на про́шлой неде́ле	last week
две неде́ли тому́ наза́д	two weeks ago
в про́шлом ме́сяце	last month
в про́шлом году́	last year
позавчера́	day before yesterday
вчера́ ве́чером	yesterday evening
за́втра у́тром	tomorrow morning
три дня тому́ наза́д	three days ago
ме́сяц тому́ наза́д	a month ago

QUIZ 4

Match the English column to the Russian.

1. среда́		a.	in the evening
2. семь		b.	north
3. март		c.	tomorrow
4. сего́дня		d.	Thank you.
5. Как дела́?		e.	Well, thank you.
6. ве́чером		f.	Good evening.
7. день		g.	Tuesday
8. се́вер		h.	Wednesday
9. вто́рник		i.	Monday
10. октя́брь		j.	winter
11. спаси́бо		k.	seven
12. восто́к		l.	in the morning
13. ле́то		m.	impossible [one may not]
14. До́брый ве́чер		n.	today
15. нельзя́		o.	summer
16. за́втра		p.	March
17. у́тром		q.	east
18. понеде́льник		r.	day
19. зима́		s.	October
20. Спаси́бо, хорошо́.		t.	How are you?

ANSWERS
1-h; 2-k; 3-p; 4-n; 5-t; 6-a; 7-r; 8-b; 9-g; 10-s; 11-d; 12-q;
13-o; 14-f; 15-m; 16-c; 17-l; 18-i; 19-j; 20-e.

LESSON 13

A. COMMON VERB FORMS

Russian verbs have two conjugations. Infinitives
of most verbs belonging to the first conjugation end
with -ать or -ять. Infinitives of verbs belonging to
the second conjugation end with -еть or -ить.
Although this is true of a great number of Russian
verbs, there are many exceptions, which will be
explained as they appear in the text.

Following are typical conjugations in the present tense:

FIRST CONJUGATION

чита́ть	to read
я чита́ю	I read
ты чита́ешь	you read
он чита́ет	he reads
мы чита́ем	we read
вы чита́ете	you read
они́ чита́ют	they read
зна́ть	to know
я зна́ю	I know
ты зна́ешь	you know
он зна́ет	he knows
мы зна́ем	we know
вы зна́ете	you know
они́ зна́ют	they know
понима́ть	to understand
я понима́ю	I understand
ты понима́ешь	you understand
он понима́ет	he understands
мы понима́ем	we understand
вы понима́ете	you understand
они́ понима́ют	they understand

ду́мать	to think
я ду́маю	I think
ты ду́маешь	you think
он ду́мает	he thinks
мы ду́маем	we think
вы ду́маете	you think
они́ ду́мают	they think

писа́ть	to write
я пишу́	I write
ты пи́шешь	you write
он пи́шет	he writes
мы пи́шем	we write
вы пи́шете	you write
они́ пи́шут	they write

NOTICE

C changes to ш and the ending у in the first-person singular and third-person plural.

Verbs ending with **-нуть** in the infinitive also belong to the first conjugation:

PERFECTIVE FUTURE

верну́ть	to return, to give back
я верну́	I will return
ты вернёшь	you will return
он вернёт	he will return
мы вернём	we will return
вы вернёте	you will return
они́ верну́т	they will return

SECOND CONJUGATION

говори́ть	to talk, to speak
я говорю́	I talk
ты говори́шь	you talk
он говори́т	he talks
мы говори́м	we talk
вы говори́те	you talk
они́ говоря́т	they talk

ви́деть	to see
я ви́жу	I see
ты ви́дишь	you see
он ви́дит	he sees
мы ви́дим	we see
вы ви́дите	you see
они́ ви́дят	they see

NOTICE

Д changes to ж in the first person.

звони́ть	to call, to ring
я звоню́	I call
ты звони́шь	you call
он звони́т	he calls
мы звони́м	we call
вы звони́те	you call
они́ звоня́т	they call

Mixed Conjugation

хоте́ть	to want

я хочу́	I want
ты хо́чешь	you want
он хо́чет	he wants
мы хоти́м	we want
вы хоти́те	you want
они́ хотя́т	they want

This verb in the singular has first-conjugation endings and changes the т to ч. In the plural it has second conjugation endings.

Reflexive Verbs

Verbs ending in -сь or -ся are reflexive, with -ся usually coming after a consonant and –сь coming after a vowel. These verbs follow the general conjugation form, retaining the ся ending after consonants and –сь after vowels:

занима́ться	to study

я занима́юсь	I study
ты занима́ешься	you study
он занима́ется	he studies
мы занима́емся	we study
вы занима́етесь	you study
они́ занима́ются	they study

B. To Be Or Not To Be: Быть

1. I AM

The verb *to be* is usually omitted in the present tense:

Я дома.	I am at home.
Мой дом о́чень удо́бный.	My home is very comfortable.

2. I WAS AND I WILL BE

However, it is used in the past and future tenses:

он был	he was
она́ была́	she was
оно́ бы́ло	it was
они́ бы́ли	they were
Я был до́ма.	I was at home.
Мо́й дом был удо́бный.	My home was comfortable.
я бу́ду	I will be
ты бу́дешь	you will be
он бу́дет	he will be
мы бу́дем	we will be
вы бу́дете	you will be
они́ бу́дут	they will be
Я бу́ду до́ма за́втра.	I will be home tomorrow.
Мой но́вый дом бу́дет о́чень удо́бный.	My new house will be very comfortable.

3. "To Be" as an Auxiliary

Быть (to be) is also used as an auxiliary verb in the imperfective future:

я бу́ду	I will
ты бу́дешь чита́ть	you will read
он бу́дет говори́ть	he will talk
они́ бу́дут писа́ть	we will write
вы бу́дете etc.	you will etc.
они́ бу́дут	they will

The past tense agrees with the gender of its subject. It is formed by dropping -ть from the infinitive and adding:

л	*(Masculine)*
ла	*(Feminine)*
ло	*(Neuter)*
ли	*(Plural)*

чита́-ть, висе́-ть

он чита́л	he was reading
она́ чита́ла	she was reading
пальто́ висе́ло	the coat was hanging
они́ чита́ли	they were reading

C. Word Study

и́мя	name
получа́ть-получи́ть	to receive
до́лго	for a long time
приве́т	greeting
за́втра	tomorrow

знамени́тый	famous
гро́мко	loudly
вре́мя	time
бога́тый	rich
коне́чно	of course

LESSON 14

A. HAVE AND HAVE NOT

Есть у вас маши́на?	Have you a car?
У неё нет маши́ны.	She doesn't have a car.
У меня́ есть каранда́ш.	I have a pencil.
У меня́ нет карандаша́.	I don't have a pencil.
Есть у тебя́ газе́та?	Do you have a newspaper?
У тебя́ нет газе́ты.	You don't have a newspaper.
У него́ есть жена́ и сын.	He has a wife and a son.
У неё нет му́жа.	She has no husband.
У вас нет де́нег.	You don't have (any) money.
У вас есть ка́рта Москвы́?	Do you have a map of Moscow?
У вас нет ка́рты Москвы́.	You don't have a map of Moscow.
У них нет вре́мени.	They don't have time.
У меня́ есть вре́мя.	I have time.
У меня́ нет вре́мени.	I don't have time.

Вот хоро́ший магази́н; у них есть всё, что вам ну́жно.	Here's a good store; they have everything you need.
Вот мо́й друг.	Here is my friend.
У него́ нет друзе́й.	He has no friends.
У вас есть сигаре́ты?	Do you have cigarettes?
У меня́ нет спи́чек.	I don't have (any) matches.
У кого́ есть спи́чки?	Who has matches?

NOTICE

1. In Russian possession is usually expressed by the following form:

у меня́ есть	I have [by me is]
у тебя́ есть	you have [by you is *fam.*]
у него́ есть	he has [by him is]
у неё есть	she has [by her is]
у нас есть	we have [by us is]
у вас есть	you have [by you is *pl.* and *pol. sing.*]
у них есть	they have [by them is]

2. When the negative is used, the object of the negative is in the genitive case:

У меня́ нет карандаша́.	I do not have a pencil.[By me is not a pencil.]
У вас нет сестры́.	You do not have a sister. [By you is not a sister.]

3. If you want to know if someone has the thing you are looking for or the thing you need, use the word есть. However, if you want to know who has the thing which you know is here, then omit the verb есть.

B. TO WANT AND TO FEEL LIKE

These are impersonal verb forms and adverb forms with the dative:

1. "To want" is expressed by the verb хотéть.

2. "To feel like" is expressed by the reflexive verb хóчется with the dative case:

Он хóчет есть.	He is hungry. [He wants to eat.]
Я хочý пить.	I want a (to) drink.
Мне хóчется пить.	I'm thirsty. [I feel like drinking.]
Мы хотúм читáть.	We want to read.
Они хотя́т спать.	They want to sleep.
Мне хóчется...	I feel like [to me it is wanting].
Мне хóчется спать.	I feel like sleeping.
Емý хóчется есть.	He feels like eating.
Им хóчется пойти́ в кинó.	They feel like going to the movies.

3. The same form and construction are used with the following verbs:

нрáвиться	to please, to like
казáться	to seem
Мне нрáвится э́тот гóрод.	I like this city. [To me is pleasing this city.]

Мне ка́жется,	It seems to me that I
что я вас зна́ю.	know you. [To me
	it seems, etc.]

4. The same form and construction are used with the following adverbs:

хо́лодно	cold
жа́рко	hot
тепло́	warm
прия́тно	pleasant
легко́	easy
интере́сно	interesting
стра́нно	strange

Мне хо́лодно.	I am cold. [To me it is cold.]
Ему́ жа́рко.	He is hot. [To him it is hot.]
Ей тепло́.	She is warm. [To her it is warm.]
Мне прия́тно.	I am glad. [To me it is pleasant.]
Нам легко́.	It is easy for us. [To us it is easy.]
Мне интере́сно.	I am interested.[To me it is interesting.]

C. Personal Pronouns with Prepositions

All forms of personal pronouns beginning with vowels take the letter **н** when used with prepositions:

у него́ есть	he has
Мы зашли́ к нему́.	We went to see him.
Я рабо́тала с ни́ми.	I worked with them.

However, when **его, её** and **их** are employed as adjectives, they do not take the **н** when used with prepositions:

у его брáта есть	his brother has
Мы зашли́ в их но́вый дом.	We went to their new house.
Она́ пришла́ с её сестро́й.	She came with her sister.

QUIZ 5

1. У него́ есть маши́на.	a. They have no time.
2. Ей здесь хо́лодно.	b. I feel like sleeping.
3. Вот моя́ кни́га.	c. He has no wife.
4. У них нет вре́мени.	d. It is their son.
5. Это их сын.	e. It's hot here.
6. Мне хо́чется спать.	f. She is cold here.
7. Тут жáрко.	g. Who has matches?
8. Это о́чень далеко́.	h. Here is my book.
9. У него́ нет жены́.	i. He has a car.
10. У кого́ есть спи́чки?	j. It's very far.

ANSWERS

1-i; 2-f; 3-h; 4-a; 5-d; 6-b; 7-e; 8-j; 9-c; 10-g.

LESSON 15

A. Do you speak Russian?

A general (yes/no) question in Russian is expressed mostly by intonation, not by any particular construction of the sentence. "Do you speak Russian?" in Russian is **Вы говори́те по-ру́сски?** [You speak by-Russian?] The answer is: **Говорю́** (Speak.) You do not have to use the pronoun *I* (**я**), since the ending of the verb **говорю** indicates the first person singular. Other questions in Russian are formed with the help of question words (see Lessons 16 and 17).

Вы говори́те по-ру́сски?	Do you speak Russian?
Да, немно́го.	Yes, a little.
Не о́чень хорошо́.	Not very well.
Я говорю́ по-ру́сски.	I speak Russian.
Он говори́т по-англи́йски.	He speaks English.
Я говорю́ о́чень пло́хо.	I speak very badly.
Мы говори́м по-ру́сски о́чень ме́дленно.	We speak Russian very slowly.
Я зна́ю то́лько не́сколько слов.	I know only a few words.
Я могу́ сказа́ть то́лько не́сколько слов по-ру́сски.	I can say only a few words in Russian.
Ваш друг говори́т по-ру́сски?	Does your friend speak Russian?
Нет, не говори́т.	No, he doesn't.
Вы понима́ете по-русски?	Do you understand Russian?
Да, понима́ю.	Yes, I understand (it).
Да, понима́ю, но не говорю́.	Yes, I understand but don't speak (it).
Я чита́ю, но не говорю́.	I read but do not speak (it).
Они́ понима́ют по-ру́сски о́чень хорошо́.	They understand Russian very well.

Вы плóхо произнóсите рýсские словá.	You pronounce Russian words badly.
Это óчень трýдное слóво.	That's a very difficult word.
Мне нужнá прáктика.	I need practice.
Вы понимáете меня?	Do you understand me?
Да, я вас понимáю.	Yes, I understand you.
Нет, я вас не понимáю.	No, I don't understand you.
Что вы сказáли?	What did you say?
Вы говорúте слúшком бы́стро.	You speak too fast.
Не говорúте так бы́стро.	Don't talk so fast.
Мне трýдно понимáть, когда вы говорúте так бы́стро.	It's difficult for me to understand when you speak so fast.
Говорúте мéдленнее.	Speak more slowly.
Пожáлуйста, говорúте немнóго мéдленнее.	Please speak a little more slowly.
Простúте, но я не понимáю вас.	Excuse me, but I don't understand you.
Пожáлуйста, повторúте.	Please repeat.
Вы понимáете меня тепéрь?	Do you understand me now?
Да, тепéрь я понимáю.	Yes, now I understand.
Я хочý хорошó	I want to speak Russian

| говори́ть по-ру́сски. | well. |
| Вы говори́те по-англи́йски? | Do you speak English? |

B. The Weather

Кака́я сего́дня пого́да?	What's the weather today?
Идёт дождь.	It's raining.
Идёт снег.	It's snowing.
Сейча́с хо́лодно.	It's cold.
Сейча́с па́смурно.	It's cloudy.
Сейча́с тепло́.	It's warm.
Сейча́с прия́тно.	It's nice.
Сейча́с жа́рко.	It's hot.
Сейча́с со́лнечно.	It's sunny.
Сейча́с ве́трено.	It's windy.
Како́й прогно́з на за́втра?	What's the forecast for tomorrow?

C. Word Study

ве́жливый	polite
бе́дный	poor
брать-взять	to take
дорого́й	expensive, dear
жизнь	life
ве́чер	evening
весёлый	cheerful
ско́лько	how much
опя́ть	again
ма́ло	little
нау́ка	science

QUIZ 6

Fill in the correct Russian word which corresponds to the English.

1. Вы _____ по-русски? Do you speak Russian?
2. Я _____ но не _____. I understand, but don't speak.
3. _____ медленнее. Speak more slowly.
4. Что вы _____ ? What did you say?
5. Я _____ только несколько слов. I know only a few words.
6. Она _____ по-русски очень _____. She reads Russian very well.
7. Сейчас _____. It's cold.
8. Не говорите так _____. Don't talk so fast.
9. _____, но я вас не понимаю. Excuse me, but I don't understand you.
10. Какая сегодня _____? What's the weather today?

ANSWERS

1. говорите; 2. понимаю, говорю; 3. говорите; 4. сказали; 5. знаю; 6. читает, хорошо; 7. холодно; 8. быстро; 9. простите; 10. погода.

LESSON 16

A. WHAT, WHICH AND WHERE

Кото́рый сейча́с час?	What time is it now?
В кото́ром часу́?	At what time?
Вот кни́га, кото́рую я чита́л.	Here is the book that I was reading.
Кото́рый раз я вам э́то говорю́?	How often have I told you that?

Де́ло, кото́рое он на́чал, идёт хорошо́.	The business that he started is going well.
Како́й э́то краси́вый язы́к!	What a pretty language this is!
Кака́я сего́дня пого́да?	What kind of weather is it today?
Каку́ю кни́гу вы чита́ете?	What book are you reading?
О како́й кни́ге вы говори́ли?	What book were you talking about?
Како́е сего́дня число́?	What is the date today?
Како́е вино́ вы хоти́те: кра́сное и́ли бе́лое?	Which wine do you want: red or white?
Како́й он у́мный!	How clever he is!
Да́йте мне каку́ю-нибу́дь кни́гу.	Give me any book.
Како́й вы стра́нный челове́к.	What a strange person you are!
Кака́я она́ краси́вая де́вушка.	What a pretty girl she is!
Куда́ вы идёте?	Where are you going?
Я иду́ на рабо́ту.	I'm going to the office (to work).
Где ва́ша рабо́та?	Where is your office (work)?
Я рабо́таю на Театра́льной пло́щади.	I work on Theatre Square.
Что на столе́?	What is on the table (location)?
На столе́ кни́ги, бума́га и каранда́ш.	Books, paper, and a pencil are on the table.

Куда́ вы положи́ли мою́ кни́гу?	Where did you put my book?
На стол.	On the table (direction).
Куда́ вы идёте обе́дать по́сле рабо́ты?	Where are you going to have dinner (to dine) after work?
Я иду́ домо́й.	I'm going home.
Я бу́ду обе́дать до́ма.	I will have dinner at home.
Отку́да вы?	Where are you from?
Я из Петербу́рга.	I'm from St. Petersburg.
Да что вы!	You don't say!
Я то́же отту́да.	I'm also from there.
Како́е совпаде́ние! Удиви́тельно!	What a coincidence! Amazing!

B. Which, What

$$\left.\begin{array}{l} \text{кото́рый, кото́рая,} \\ \text{кото́рое, кото́рые} \\ \text{како́й, кака́я,} \\ \text{како́е, каки́е} \end{array}\right\} \text{which, what}$$

"Which" and "what" are declined like adjectives and must agree in gender, number, and case with the nouns they modify.

Како́й краси́вый дом!	What a pretty house!

Here дом is masculine, nominative, and singular; so is како́й.

На каку́ю карти́ну вы смо́трите?	Which picture are you looking at?

Картину is feminine, accusative, and singular; so is какую.

| О каки́х кни́гах
вы говори́ли? | Which books were you
talking about? |

Кни́гах is feminine, plural, and prepositional; so is каки́х.

C. WHERE WITH THE ACCUSATIVE AND PREPOSITIONAL.

"Where" in Russian is rendered by:

Куда́ "where to," "whither" (direction) is always used with the acccusative case.

Где "where is" (location) is always used with the prepositional case.

Я иду́ в шко́лу.	I go to school.
идти́ в шко́лу	to go to (direction)
Я рабо́таю в шко́ле.	I work in (the) school
рабо́тать в шко́ле	to work in (location)
Кни́гу положи́ли на стол.	They put the book on the table.
положи́ть на стол	to put on (direction)
Кни́га лежи́т на столе́.	The book is lying on the table.
лежа́ть на столе́	to lie on (location)

QUIZ 7

1. _____ это краси́вый язы́к! What a pretty language this is!
2. _____ вы идёте по́сле рабо́ты? Where are you going after work?
3. _____ ва́ша рабо́та? Where is your office?
4. _____ вы положи́ли мою́ кни́гу? Where did you put my book?

5. О _____ книге вы говорите? What book you are talking about?
6. Книга, _____ я читал. The book which I was reading.
7. Я положил её _____. I put it on the table.
8. Дайте мне _____ книгу. Give me any book.
9. _____ она умная! How clever she is!
10. _____ это красивое пальто! What a beautiful coat this is!

ANSWERS
1. какой; 2. куда; 3. где; 4. куда; 5. какой; 6. которую; 7. на стол; 8. какую-нибудь; 9. какая; 10. какое.

LESSON 17

A. WHOSE?

Чей это дом?	Whose house is that?
Чей это карандаш?	Whose pencil is that?
Чья это книга?	Whose book is that?
Чья газета там на столе?	Whose newspaper is [there] on the table?
Чьё это пальто?	Whose coat is that?
Чьи это дети?	Whose children are these?
Чьи деньги она тратит?	Whose money does she spend?

Чей, чья, чьё, чьи (whose) agree in gender, number, and case with nouns they modify:

Чья книга?	Whose book?

Книга is feminine and nominative; so is чья.

| На чью книгу вы смотрите? | Whose book are you looking at? |

Книгу is femine and accusative; so is чью.

| Чьим карандашом вы пишете? | Whose pencil are you writing with? |

Карандашом is masculine and instrumental; so is чьим.

	MASC.	FEM.	NEUT.	PLUR. ALL GEND.
Nom.	чей	чья	чьё	чьи
Gen.	чьего	чьей	чьего	чьих
Dat.	чьему	чьей	чьему	чьим
Acc.	чей or чьего	чью	чьё	чьи or чьих
Inst.	чьим	чьей(ею)	чьим	чьими
Prep.	о чьём	о чьей	о чьём	о чьих

B. What, How

Как вас зовут?	What is your name? [How are you called?]
Как ваше имя?	What is your name?
Как её зовут?	What is her name?
Как дела?	How are things?
Как по-русски...?	What is the Russian for...?
Как это пишется?	How is that spelled?
Как называется эта книга?	What is the name of this book?
Как называется этот город?	What is the name of this city?
Как пройти на улицу Горького?	How do you get to Gorky Street?

Как вы ду́маете– он хорошо́ говори́т по-ру́сски?	What do you think– does he speak Russian well?
Как хорошо́ он говори́т по-ру́сски!	How well he speaks Russian!
Как здесь жа́рко!	How hot it is here!
Как вам нра́вится Москва́?	How do you like Moscow?
Как вам не сты́дно так бы́стро забы́ть меня́!	Aren't you ashamed to have forgotten me so fast?
Как я ра́да, что встре́тила вас!	How glad I am that I met you!
Вот как!	Is that so!
Как прия́тно гуля́ть в саду́!	How pleasant it is to stroll in the garden!
Как ни стара́йтесь– ничего́ не вы́йдет.	No matter how you try, nothing will come of it.
Как бы не так!	Nothing of the sort!
Бу́дьте как до́ма.	Make yourself at home.
с тех пор, как	since
как ви́дно	apparently [as it is seen]
Это как раз то, что мне ну́жно!	It's just the thing I need!

C. THE DEMONSTRATIVE PRONOUN Это

Note the difference between: э́то, meaning "this is," "that is," and э́тот, э́та, э́то, meaning "this."

Э́то каранда́ш.	This is a pencil.
Э́тот каранда́ш мой.	This pencil is mine.

Э́то кни́га.	This is a book.
Э́та кни́га не моя́.	This book is not mine.

D. WORD STUDY

переводи́ть-перевести́	to translate
симпати́чный	nice
о́коло	near
фотогра́фия	photograph
коне́ц	end
изуча́ть-изучи́ть	to study in depth
тёплый	warm
ве́тер	wind
страна́	country
доро́га	road

QUIZ 8

1. Как называ́ется э́тот го́род?
2. Как вам не сты́дно так ско́ро забы́ть меня́?!
3. Как дела́?
4. Бу́дьте как до́ма.
5. Как бы не так!
6. Чьи э́ти де́ти?
7. Чей это каранда́ш?
8. Как прия́тно гуля́ть в саду́!
9. Как вас зову́т?
10. Как это пи́шется?
11. Как здесь жа́рко!
12. Как дойти́ до у́лицы Го́рького?
13. Чей э́то дом?
14. Вот как!
15. Как по-ру́сски...?
16. Как называ́ется э́та кни́га?
17. Как я рад, что встре́тил вас!

a. How pleasant it is to stroll in the garden!
b. What is the Russian for...?
c. Make yourself at home.
d. Whose children are these?
e. How hot it is here!
f. What is your name?
g. Whose house is this?
h. How do you get to Gorky Street?
i. Is that so!
j. What is the name of this city!
k. How are things?
l. Whose pencil is that?
m. What is the name of this book?
n. Aren't you ashamed to have forgotten me so soon?
o. How glad I am that I met you!

18. Как вы ду́маете–он
    хорошо́ говори́т
    по-ру́сски?

p. What do you think—does
   he speak Russian well?
q. How is that spelled?
r. Nothing of the sort!

ANSWERS
1-j; 2-n; 3-k; 4-c; 5-r; 6-d; 7-l; 8-a; 9-f; 10-q; 11-e; 12-h;
13-g; 14-i; 15-b; 16-m; 17-o; 18-p.

LESSON 18

A. MEETING A FRIEND

До́брое у́тро.	Good morning.
Здра́вствуйте.	Hello.
Вы говори́те по-ру́сски?	Do you speak Russian?
Да, я говорю́ по-ру́сски.	Yes, I speak Russian.
А я не говорю́ по-англи́йски.	I don't speak English.
Вы с ю́га?	Are you from the south?
Да, я из Кры́ма.	Yes, I'm from the Crimea.
Как давно́ (or ско́лько вре́мени) вы уже́ в Соединённых Шта́тах?	How long (how much time) have you been in the United States?
Два ме́сяца.	Two months.
Вы бы́стро вы́учите англи́йский язы́к.	You will learn English quickly.
Э́тот язы́к не о́чень тру́дный.	This language is not very difficult.
Он гора́здо трудне́е, чем вы ду́маете.	It's far more difficult than you think.

Возмо́жно, вы пра́вы. Наве́рно, нам гора́здо ле́гче вы́учить ру́сский язы́к, чем вам вы́учить англи́йский.	You may be right. It's probably much easier for us to learn Russian than for you to learn English.
Вы говори́те по-ру́сски о́чень хорошо́.	You speak Russian very well.
Я жил в Крыму́ не́сколько лет.	I lived in the Crimea for several years.
У вас прекра́сное произноше́ние.	Your pronunciation is excellent. [You have excellent pronunciation.]
Спаси́бо, но всё же мне ну́жно бо́льше говори́ть (ог мне нужна́ пра́ктика).	Thank you, but all the same I need to speak more [I need practice].
Мне ну́жно идти́. Мой по́езд сейча́с отхо́дит.	I have to go. My train is leaving immediately.
Всего́ хоро́шего и счастли́вого пути́.	All the best, and have a pleasant trip.
Жела́ю и вам того́ же. До свида́ния.	The same to you. Good-bye.
До свида́ния.	Good-bye.

QUIZ 9

Choose the correct word:

1. Она _____ (speaks) по-русски.
   a. говорю
   b. читает
   c. говорит

2. Я _____ (don't speak) по-англи́йски.
   a. чита́ю
   b. не говорю́
   c. говори́т

3. Я _____ (lived) в Крыму́.
   a. рабо́таю
   b. жить
   c. жил

4. Ру́сский _____ (easier) чем англи́йский.
   a. ле́гче
   b. бо́льше
   c. хорошо́

5. Кака́я _____ (today) пого́да?
   a. за́втра
   b. вчера́
   c. сего́дня

6. Как называ́ется э́тот _____ (city)?
   a. кни́га
   b. го́род
   c. у́лица

7. Я иду́ _____ (home).
   a. до́ма
   b. домо́й
   c. в до́ме

8. Куда́ вы _____ (are going)?
   a. иду́
   b. идёт
   c. идёте

9. _____ (What) сего́дня число́?
   a. Како́е
   b. Что
   c. Как

10. _____ (Which) тепе́рь час?
    a. Како́е
    b. Кото́рый
    c. Каку́ю

11. _____ (Where) ваша работа?
   a. Где
   b. Куда
   c. Как

12. _____ (Where) вы положили книгу?
   a. Где
   b. Куда
   c. Как

13. Вы говорите слишком _____ (fast).
   a. плохо
   b. быстро
   c. тихо

14. Я _____ (you) не понимаю.
   a. вам
   b. вы
   c. вас

15. _____ (he has) нет друзей.
   a. У него
   b. У меня
   c. У вас

16. _____ (She has) нет мужа.
   a. У меня
   b. У неё
   c. У него

17. _____ (I am) холодно.
   a. Мне
   b. Ему
   c. Вам

18. _____ (She is) жарко.
   a. Мне
   b. Ей
   c. Её

19. Вот _____ (good) магазин.
   a. хороший
   b. добрый
   c. плохой

20. Они _____ (want) спать.
   a. хочу
   b. хочешь
   c. хотят

ANSWERS
1-c; 2-b; 3-c; 4-a; 5-c; 6-b; 7-b; 8-c; 9-a; 10-b; 11-a; 12-b; 13-b;
14-c; 15-a; 16-b; 17-a; 18-b; 19-a; 20-c.

B. Introductions

1. Pleased to Meet You

Разреши́те предста́виться.	Allow me to introduce myself.
Меня́ зову́т Ива́н.	My name is John.
Меня зову́т Мари́я.	My name is Mary.
О́чень прия́тно.	Pleased to meet you.
Я хоте́ла бы предста́вить вас Игорю.	I'd like to introduce you to Igor.
Отку́да вы?	Where are you from?
Я живу́ в США.	I live in the U.S.
Я живу́ в Англии.	I live in England.
Я в командиро́вке.	I'm here on a business trip.

2. Are You Here on Vacation?

До́брый день!	Hello!
Разреши́те предста́виться.	Allow me to introduce myself.
Меня́ зову́т Джейн Бра́ун.	My name is Jane Brown.
О́чень прия́тно с ва́ми познако́миться.	Pleased to meet you.
Меня́ зову́т Ива́н Семёнов.	My name is Ivan Semyonov.
О́чень прия́тно.	Pleased to meet you.

Вы здесь в отпуску?	Are you here on vacation?
Да. Я буду в Москве ещё четыре дня.	Yes. I'll be here in Moscow another four days.
Желаю вам приятно провести время!	Have a pleasant time!

C. Word Study

современный	contemporary
начало	beginning
портрет	portrait
правильно	correctly
любить	to love
везде	everywhere
рад	glad (adj.)
трудный	difficult
мир	world, peace

LESSON 19

A. Cardinal Numerals

один	one
два	two
три	three
четыре	four
пять	five
шесть	six
семь	seven
восемь	eight
девять	nine
десять	ten
одиннадцать	eleven
двенадцать	twelve

трина́дцать	thirteen
четы́рнадцать	fourteen
пятна́дцать	fifteen
шестна́дцать	sixteen
семна́дцать	seventeen
восемна́дцать	eighteen
девятна́дцать	nineteen
два́дцать	twenty
два́дцать оди́н	twenty-one
два́дцать два	twenty-two
два́дцать три	twenty-three
три́дцать	thirty
три́дцать оди́н	thirty-one
три́дцать два	thirty-two
три́дцать три	thirty-three
со́рок	forty
со́рок оди́н	forty-one
со́рок два	forty-two
со́рок три	forty-three
пятьдеся́т	fifty
пятьдеся́т оди́н	fifty-one
пятьдеся́т два	fifty-two
пятьдеся́т три	fifty-three
шестьдеся́т	sixty
шестьдеся́т оди́н	sixty-one
шестьдеся́т два	sixty-two
шестьдеся́т три	sixty-three
се́мьдесят	seventy
се́мьдесят оди́н	seventy-one
се́мьдесят два	seventy-two
се́мьдесят три	seventy-three
во́семьдесят	eighty
во́семьдесят оди́н	eighty-one
во́семьдесят два	eighty-two
во́семьдесят три	eighty-three
девяно́сто	ninety

девяносто один	ninety-one
девяносто два	ninety-two
девяносто три	ninety-three
сто	one hundred
сто один	one hundred and one
сто два	one hundred and two
сто три	one hundred and three
сто двадцать	one hundred and twenty
сто тридцать	one hundred and thirty
сто тридцать один	one hundred and thirty-one
сто тридцать два	one hundred and thirty-two
сто тридцать три	one hundred and thirty-three
двести	two hundred
триста	three hundred
четыреста	four hundred
пятьсот	five hundred
шестьсот	six hundred
семьсот	seven hundred
восемьсот	eight hundred
девятьсот	nine hundred
тысяча	one thousand
миллион	one million
миллиард	one billion

B. Cases with Cardinal Numerals

оди́н *(m)*, одна́ *(f.)*, одно́ *(n.)*, одни́ *(pl.)*
два *(m.)*, две *(f.)*, два *(n.)*

1. When the cardinal numeral is used in the nominative case:

The nominative singular is used after оди́н, одна́, одно́.
The nominative plural is used after одни́.

The genitive singular is used after два, две, три, четы́ре.
The genitive plural is used after пять, шесть, семь, etc.

2. When the number is compound, the case of the noun depends on the last digit:

Sing.	два́дцать оди́н каранда́ш	twenty-one pencils
Gen. *Pl.*	два́дцать два карандаша́	twenty-two pencils
Gen. *Pl.*	два́дцать пять карандаше́й	twenty-five pencils

C. DECLENSION OF NUMERALS

All cardinal numerals decline, agreeing in case with the noun they modify (with the exception of the nominative case, which is discussed above).

Gen. *Sing.*	**Я оста́лся без одно́й копе́йки.**	
	I remained with out one cent.	
Gen. *Pl.*	**Он был там оди́н ме́сяц без двух дней.**	
	He was there one month less two days.	
Dat. *Pl.*	**Мы пришли́ к пяти́ часа́м.**	
	We arrived by five o'clock.	
Prep. *Pl.*	**Они́ говоря́т о семи́ рубля́х.**	
	They are speaking about seven rubles.	

TABLE OF DECLENSION OF NUMERALS

Nom.						
оди́н-одно́	одна́	одни́	два-две	три	четы́ре	
Gen.						
одного́	одно́й	одни́х	двух	трёх	четырёх	
Dat.						
одному́	одно́й	одни́м	дву́м	трём	четырём	
Acc.						
оди́н-одно́	одну́	одни́	два-две	три	четы́ре	
одного́		одни́х	дву́х	трёх	четырёх	

Inst.

| одни́м | одно́й | одни́ми | двумя́ | тремя́ | четырьмя́ |

Prep.

| об одно́м | об одно́й | об одни́х | о дву́х | о трёх | о четырёх |

Nom.

| пять | шесть | семь | во́семь | де́вять | де́сять |

Gen.

| пяти́ | шести́ | семи́ | восьми́ | девяти́ | десяти́ |

Dat.

| пяти́ | шести́ | семи́ | восьми́ | девяти́ | десяти́ |

Acc.

| пять | шесть | семь | во́семь | де́вять | де́сять |

Inst.

| пятью́ | шестью́ | семью́ | восемью́ | девятью́ | десятью́ |

Prep.

| о пяти́ | о шести́ | о семи́ | о восьми́ | о девяти́ | о десяти́ |

QUIZ 10

1.	Девять	a.	102
2.	Двадцать один	b.	43
3.	Двенадцать	c.	600
4.	Пятьдесят	d.	30
5.	Пятнадцать	e.	1,000
6.	Сорок три	f.	5
7.	Четырнадцать	g.	9
8.	Четыреста	h.	15
9.	Сто два	i.	50
10.	Пять	j.	11
11.	Шестьсот	k.	21
12.	Тысяча	l.	80
13.	Тридцать	m.	400
14.	Одиннадцать	n.	14
15.	Восемьдесят	o.	12

ANSWERS

1-g; 2-k; 3-o; 4-i; 5-h; 6-b; 7-n; 8-m; 9-a; 10-f; 11-c; 12-e; 13-d; 14-j; 15-l.

LESSON 20

A. Ordinal Numerals

пе́рвый	first
второ́й	second
тре́тий	third
четвёртый	fourth
пя́тый	fifth
шесто́й	sixth
седьмо́й	seventh
восьмо́й	eighth
девя́тый	ninth
деся́тый	tenth
оди́ннадцатый	eleventh
двена́дцатый	twelfth
трина́дцатый	thirteenth
четы́рнадцатый	fourteenth
пятна́дцатый	fifteenth
шестна́дцатый	sixteenth
семна́дцатый	seventeenth
восемна́дцатый	eighteenth
девятна́дцатый	nineteenth
двадца́тый	twentieth
два́дцать пе́рвый	twenty-first
два́дцать второ́й	twenty-second
два́дцать тре́тий	twenty-third
тридца́тый	thirtieth
три́дцать пе́рвый	thirty-first
три́дцать второ́й	thirty-second
три́дцать тре́тий	thirty-third
сороково́й	fortieth
соро́к пе́рвый	forty-first
со́рок второ́й	forty-second
со́рок тре́тий	forty-third
пятидеся́тый	fiftieth

пятьдеся́т пе́рвый	fifty-first
пятьдеся́т второ́й	fifty-second
пятьдеся́т тре́тий	fifty-third
шестидеся́тый	sixtieth
шестьдеся́т пе́рвый	sixty-first
шестьдеся́т второ́й	sixty-second
шестьдеся́т тре́тий	sixty-third
семидеся́тый	seventieth
се́мьдесят пе́рвый	seventy-first
се́мьдесят второ́й	seventy-second
се́мьдесят тре́тий	seventy-third
восьмидеся́тый	eightieth
во́семьдесят пе́рвый	eighty-first
во́семьдесят второ́й	eighty-second
во́семьдесят тре́тий	eighty-third
девяно́стый	ninetieth
девяно́сто пе́рвый	ninety-first
девяно́сто второ́й	ninety-second
девяно́сто тре́тий	ninety-third
со́тый	hundredth
сто пе́рвый	hundred and first
сто второ́й	hundred second
сто тре́тий	hundred third
сто двадца́тый	hundred twentieth
сто тридца́тый	hundred thirtieth
сто три́дцать пе́рвый	hundred thirty-first
сто три́дцать второ́й	hundred thirty-second
сто три́дцать тре́тий	hundred thirty-third
двухсо́тый	two hundredth
трёхсо́тый	three hundredth
четырёхсо́тый [1]	four hundredth
пятисо́тый	five hundredth
шестисо́тый	six hundredth

[1] This is one of very few exceptions where one word has two stresses, and that is only because it is a compound word.

семисо́тый	seven hundredth
восьмисо́тый	eight hundredth
девятисо́тый	nine hundredth
ты́сячный	thousandth
миллио́нный	millionth
миллиа́рдный	billionth

B. CHARACTERISTICS OF ORDINAL NUMERALS

All ordinal numerals are like adjectives, and decline as such:

MASC.	FEM.	NEUT.	PLUR.
пе́рвый	пе́рвая	пе́рвое	пе́рвые
второ́й	втора́я	второ́е	вторы́е

In compound forms, only the last digit changes, and only that digit is declined:

двадца́тый век	twentieth century
Это бы́ло три́дцать пе́рвого декабря́.	That was on December 31.
тре́тий раз	third time
Втора́я мирова́я война́ ко́нчилась в ты́сяча девятьсо́т со́рок пя́том году́.	The Second World War ended in 1945 [one thousand, nine hundred, forty-fifth year].
пя́тый год пя́том году́	(prepositional singular)

C. Word Study

река́	river
кли́мат	climate
рома́н	novel
находи́ться	to be located
висе́ть	to be hanging
расска́з	story
давно́	a long time ago
холо́дный	cold
чай	tea
господи́н	Mister

LESSON 21

A. Numbers in Context

Это двадца́тый уро́к.	This is the twentieth lesson.
Я уже́ зна́ю девятна́дцать уро́ков.	I already know nineteen lessons.
Я купи́ла но́вую шля́пу за де́сять рубле́й.	I bought a new hat for ten rubles.
Мы за́втракаем в двена́дцать часо́в.	We have lunch at twelve o'clock.
Ско́лько вам лет?	How old are you?
Мне два́дцать лет.	I am twenty years old.
Ему́ два́дцать оди́н год.	He is twenty-one years old.
Ей три́дцать два го́да.	She is thirty-two years old.
Ива́ну Петро́вичу три́дцать пять лет.	Ivan Petrovich is thirty-five years old.

Я встаю́ в во́семь часо́в утра́.	I get up at eight o'clock in the morning.
Он рабо́тает с девяти́ утра́ до пяти́ часо́в ве́чера.	He works from nine in the morning until five [o'clock] in the aftenoon.
Ско́лько э́то сто́ит?	How much does this cost?
(Э́то сто́ит) пятьдеся́т рубле́й.	This costs fifty rubles.
Ско́лько сто́ит э́тот костю́м?	How much does this suit cost?
(Э́тот костю́м сто́ит) се́мьдесят пять рубле́й.	This suit costs seventy-five rubles.
Э́то о́чень до́рого.	That's very expensive.
Э́то дёшево.	That's cheap.
Да́йте мне, пожа́луйста, друго́й.	Please give me another [a different one].
Покажи́те мне, пожа́луйста, э́ту кни́гу.	Please show me this book.
Каку́ю? Э́ту?	Which? This?
Нет, не э́ту, а ту другу́ю.	No, not this, but that other.
Пожа́луйста.	Please.
Ско́лько она́ сто́ит?	How much does it (she) cost?
Де́сять рубле́й и се́мьдесят пять копе́ек.	Ten rubles and seventy-five kopecks.
Э́то не до́рого.	That's not expensive.
Я куплю́ её.	I'll buy it.
Когда́ я прие́хала в Москву́, у меня́ бы́ло две́сти рубле́й.	When I arrived in Moscow, I had two hundred rubles.

В э́той гости́нице де́вять этаже́й.	There are nine floors in this hotel.
Мой друг живёт на у́лице Пу́шкина, дом но́мер сто во́семьдесят четы́ре, кварти́ра два́дцать три.	My friend lives at 184 Pushkin Street, Apartment 23. [My friend lives on Pushkin street, house number one hundred eighty-four, apartment twenty-three.]
Его́ телефо́н 217-34-57.	His telephone number is 217-34-57.
Мой телефо́н 6-71-85.	My telephone number is 6-71-85.

B. How Old Are You?

"How old are you?" is expressed in Russian by the phrase Ско́лько вам (dative of вы) лет? [How many to you years?]

Мне два́дцать лет.	I am twenty years old. [To me twenty years.].

After 20, use the genitive plural.

Мне со́рок пять лет.	I am forty-five years old. [To me forty-five years.]

After 5, use the genitive plural.

Ему́ три́дцать оди́н год.	He is thirty-one years old. [To him thirty-one years.]

After 1, use the nominative singular.

Ей два́дцать три го́да.	She is twenty-three years old. [To her twenty-three years.]

After 3, use the genitive singular.

C. How Much, How Many

"How much?" and "how many?" are both expressed by one word in Russian: ско́лько.

Ско́лько э́то сто́ит?	How much does it cost?
Ско́лько раз я вам э́то говори́ла?	How many times have I told you that?
Ско́лько ученико́в в кла́ссе?	How many students are in the class?

After ско́лько and other adverbs of quantity—не́сколько (several), мно́го (many), ма́ло (little)—the genitive plural is always used.

QUIZ 11

1. Я купи́л но́вую шля́пу за _____ рубле́й. I bought a new hat for ten rubles.
2. Ей _____ го́да. She is thirty-two years old.
3. Я встаю́ в _____ часо́в утра́. I get up at eight o'clock in the morning.
4. У меня́ есть _____ рубле́й. I have two hundred rubles.
5. _____ сто́ит э́тот костю́м? How much does this suit cost?

6. _____ книг вы взяли домой? How many books did you take home?
7. Мой друг _____ на улице Пушкина. My friend lives on Pushkin Street.
8. Дом номер _____, квартира _____. [House] Number 184, Apartment 23.
9. В этой гостинице _____ этажей. There are nine floors in this hotel.
10. Он работает с _____ утра до _____ вечера. He works from nine in the morning until five [o'clock] in the afternoon.

ANSWERS
1. десять; 2. тридцать два; 3. восемь; 4. двести; 5. сколько; 6. сколько; 7. живёт; 8. сто восемьдесят четвёртый, двадцать третья; 9. девять этажей; 10. девяти, пяти.

LESSON 22

A. I LIKE, I DON'T LIKE

Мне о́чень нра́вится э́тот го́род.	I like this city very much.
Мне не нра́вится э́та у́лица.	I don't like this street.
Я люблю́ жить в дере́вне ле́том.	I love to live in the country during the summer.
В Нью-Йо́рке есть мно́го хоро́ших рестора́нов.	There are many good restaurants in New York.
Мне не нра́вится э́тот рестора́н.	I don't like this restaurant.
Како́й вку́сный ко́фе!	What delicious coffee!
Я всегда́ пью ко́фе с молоко́м.	I always drink coffee with milk.

Я не люблю́ молоко́.	I don't like milk.
Ко́фе без молока́ гора́здо вкусне́е.	Coffee without milk tastes much better [is much tastier].
Это де́ло вку́са.	It's a question of taste.
Како́е вку́сное пиро́жное!	What delicious pie!
Переда́йте мне, пожа́луйста, са́хар, соль, ло́жку, нож, ви́лку, хлеб.	Please pass [me] the sugar, salt, spoon, knife, fork, [and] bread.
Где моя́ салфе́тка?	Where is my napkin?

B. Telling Time

Telling time in Russian is rather complicated, but the simple form—два пятна́дцать (2:15), пять со́рок пять (5:45)—may always be used. Russians say:

2:05–пять мину́т тре́тьего (genitive of тре́тий)	five minutes of the third hour
2:55–без пяти́ три	without five: three
3:30–полови́на четвёртого (genitive of четвёртый)	half of the fourth
7:40–без двадцати́ во́семь	without twenty: eight
7:00 A.M.–семь часо́в утра́	seven o'clock in the morning
7:00 P.M.–семь часо́в ве́чера	seven o'clock in the evening
Ско́лько сейча́с вре́мени? (Кото́рый час?)	What time is it now? [Which is now the hour?]

Во ско́лько (в кото́ром часу́) отхо́дит по́езд?	When [at what hour] does the train leave?
Сейча́с двена́дцать часо́в дня, час дня.	It's now twelve noon, one o'clock in the afternoon.
Де́сять мину́т пя́того.	Ten minutes after four [ten minutes of the fifth (hour)].
Без че́тверти шесть.	A quarter [without a quarter] of six.
Де́сять часо́в утра́.	Ten o'clock in the morning.
Семь часо́в ве́чера.	Seven o'clock in the evening.
По́лдень.	Noon.
По́лночь.	Midnight.
Полови́на пе́рвого.	Half-past twelve.
Полови́на второ́го.	Half-past one.
Че́тверть тре́тьего.	A quarter after two [a quarter of the third].
Спекта́кль начина́ется без че́тверти во́семь.	The performance starts at a quarter of eight.
Эта кни́га была́ напи́сана в ты́сяча девятьсо́т во́семьдесят пя́том году́.	This book was written in 1985 [one thousand, nine hundred, eighty-fifth year].

NOTICE

After **без** (without), the genitive is used.

Мои́ часы́ отстаю́т.	My watch is slow.
Мои́ часы́ спеша́т.	My watch is fast.
Мои́ часы́ стоя́т.	My watch isn't going. [has stopped].

NOTICE

Часы (watch or clock) is always used in the plural and takes a plural verb.

C. COMPARATIVE OF ADJECTIVES

To form the comparative of an adjective, drop the gender ending and add ee for all gender endings and the plural. The adjective does not decline in the comparative:

краси́вый	pretty
краси́в-ее	prettier
тёплый	warm
тепл-е́е	warmer
весёлый	merry
весел-е́е	merrier

Irregular comparative forms:

хоро́ший	good
лу́чше	better
большо́й	big
бо́льше	bigger
ма́ленький	small
ме́ньше	smaller
широ́кий	wide
ши́ре	wider
у́зкий	narrow
у́же	narrower
плохо́й	bad
ху́же	worse
высо́кий	tall
вы́ше	taller
ти́хий	quiet
ти́ше	quieter

дорого́й	dear
доро́же	dearer
просто́й	simple
про́ще	simpler
то́лстый	fat
то́лще	fatter

Москва́ бо́льше чем Ха́рьков.	Moscow is larger than Kharkov.
Во́лга длинне́е Днепра́.	The Volga is longer than the Dnieper.
Нью-Йо́рк са́мый большо́й го́род в ми́ре.	New York is the largest city in the world.
Здесь (о́чень) хо́лодно.	It's (very) cold here.
Сего́дня холодне́е, чем вчера́.	It's colder today than yesterday.
Вчера́ бы́ло о́чень тепло́.	It was very warm yesterday.
Зимо́й на ю́ге тепле́е, чем на се́вере.	In the winter it's warmer in the south than in the north.
Там, где мы бы́ли вчера́, тепле́е, вкусне́е гото́вят и вообще́ лу́чше.	The place we were yesterday is warmer, they prepared food better, and it's better in general.
Пойде́мте туда́.	Let's go there.

D. SUPERLATIVE OF ADJECTIVES

The superlative of adjectives has two forms. The simpler form is made up by adding са́мый, са́мая, са́мое, or са́мые (the most) to the adjective. For instance:

са́мый большо́й	the biggest
са́мая краси́вая	the prettiest
са́мые у́мные	the most clever

Са́мый declines with the adjective:

в са́мом большо́м до́ме	in the very largest house
Он пришёл с са́мой краси́вой же́нщиной.	He came with the prettiest woman.

QUIZ 12

1. Сего́дня холодне́е, чем вчера́.
2. Я люблю́ жить в дере́вне ле́том.
3. Я бо́льше, чем мой брат.
4. Како́й го́род са́мый большо́й в ми́ре?
5. Там, где мы бы́ли вчера́, тепле́е, вкусне́е и лу́чше.
6. Она́ всегда́ пьёт ко́фе с молоко́м.
7. Переда́йте мне, пожа́луйста, са́хар.
8. Ко́фе без молока́ гора́здо вкусне́е.
9. Ско́лько сейча́с вре́мени?
10. (Когда́) во ско́лько вы бу́дете до́ма?
11. Де́сять мину́т пя́того.
12. Без десяти́ шесть.
13. Полови́на пе́рвого.
14. Конце́рт начина́ется без че́тверти во́семь.
15. Семь часо́в ве́чера.

a. Where we were yesteday is warmer, tastier, and better.
b. Pass [me] the sugar, please.
c. What time is it now?
d. Half-past twelve
e. The concert starts at a quarter to eight.
f. Coffee without milk tastes much better.
g. Ten minutes to six
h. It's colder today than yesterday.
i. Which city is the largest in the world?
j. I love to live in the country in the summer.
k. She always drinks coffee with milk.
l. Ten minutes past four.
m. Seven P.M.
n. I am bigger than my brother.
o. When [at what time] will you be home?

ANSWERS
1–h, 2–j, 3–n, 4–i, 5–a, 6–k, 7–b, 8–f, 9–c, 10–o, 11–l, 12–g, 13–d, 14–e, 15–m.

LESSON 23

A. NEGATIVES

Я ничего́ не зна́ю.	I don't know anything.
Он ничего́ не хо́чет де́лать.	He doesn't want to do anything.
Не на́до ему́ ничего́ говори́ть.	Don't tell him anything.
Мне ничего́ не на́до.	I don't need anything.
Она́ никуда́ не хо́чет идти́.	She doesn't want to go anywhere.
Они́ никогда́ не говоря́т, куда́ они́ иду́т.	They never say where they are going.
Тут о́чень темно́, я ничего́ не ви́жу.	It's very dark here; I don't see anything.
Никто́ не зна́ет, как дойти́ до библиоте́ки.	No one knows how to get to the library.
Я был в магази́не и ничего́ не купи́л.	I was in the store but didn't buy anything.
Я ещё нигде́ не был.	I haven't been anywhere yet.
Мы здесь уже́ две неде́ли и ещё не получи́ли ни одного́ письма́.	We have already been here two weeks and still haven't received one letter.

NOTICE

A second (double) negative must be used with the following
words:

ничего́	nothing
никто́	nobody
никогда́	never
никуда́	nowhere

I nothing	don't	(verb).
Я ничего́	не	хочу́, знаю.
Nobody	doesn't	(verb).
Никто́	не	ви́дит, говори́т.
Never	don't	(verb).
Он никогда́	не	был в Москве́.
Мы никогда́	не	говори́м по-ру́сски.

A negative adverb or pronoun must also use a
negative with the verb it modifies. Negative
words with не, on the other hand (не́чего, не́кого,
не́когда, не́где, не́куда), are not used with a
negated verb:

Мне	не́где	жить.
(To me)	nowhere	to live.
Мне	не́когда	чита́ть
(To me)	no time	to read.
Мне	не́куда	идти́.
(To me)	nowhere	to go.

B. Predicative Form of Adjectives

Qualitative adjectives have two forms: the regular, which is called long, and a short form, so called because its ending is shortened. The masculine ends in a hard consonant, the feminine in **a**, neuter in **o** or **e**, and plural in **ы** or **и**.

Long		Short		
	Masc.	Fem.	Neuter	Plural
ста́рый	стар	стара́	ста́ро	ста́ры

This short form is used only as a predicate:

Эта ста́рая кни́га лежи́т на столе́.	This old book is lying on the table.
Он стар.	He is old (predicate).

C. Asking Directions

Я иностра́нец.	I'm a foreigner.
Я ничего́ не зна́ю в э́том го́роде.	I don't know anything about [in] this city.
Скажи́те, пожа́луйста, где здесь по́чта.	Please tell me where the post office is.
Два кварта́ла пря́мо, пото́м оди́н кварта́л напра́во.	Two blocks straight ahead, then one block to the right.
Большо́й дом на углу́, э́то по́чта.	The big building on the corner–that's the post office.
А что это за дом нале́во?	And what is this building on the left?
Это библиоте́ка.	That's the library.

Вы не зна́ете, где нахо́дится Большо́й теа́тр?	Do you know where the Bolshoi Theatre is?
Да, зна́ю.	Yes, I know.
Как туда́ прое́хать?	How do you get there?
Вам ну́жно сесть на тролле́йбус и прое́хать три остано́вки.	You have to take a trolleybus and go three stops.
Сойди́те на Театра́льной пло́щади, и там вы уви́дите Большо́й теа́тр.	Get off at Theatre Square, and there you'll see the Bolshoi Theatre.
А где остано́вка тролле́йбуса?	And where is the trolleybus stop?
На той стороне́ у́лицы. Вы мо́жете перейти́ на ту сто́рону то́лько когда́ зелёный свет.	On that side of the street. You can cross to the other side only when the light is green.
Как ча́сто хо́дят тролле́йбусы?	How often do the trolleybuses run?
Ка́ждые пять мину́т.	Every five minutes.
Все тролле́йбусы на э́той остано́вке иду́т к Большо́му теа́тру?	Do all trolleybuses at that stop go to the Bolshoi Theatre?
Нет. То́лько тролле́йбус № 10. Девя́тый но́мер идёт на вокза́л, а семна́дцатый в аэропо́рт.	No. Only trolleybus Number 10. Number 9 goes to the railroad station, and Number 17 goes to the airport.
Вы не зна́ете, что сего́дня идёт в Большо́м теа́тре?	And do [would] you know what is playing today at the Bolshoi Theatre?

Как же! Коне́чно зна́ю! Идёт «Лебеди́ное о́зеро».	What a question! Of course I do! *Swan Lake* is playing.
Что вы говори́те! Я давно́ хоте́л посмотре́ть э́тот бале́т.	You don't say! I've wanted to see that ballet for a long time.
Большо́е спаси́бо.	Thanks a lot.
Очень вам благода́рен.	I'm very grateful to you.
Пожа́луйста.	You're welcome.

QUIZ 13

1. Он ничего не знает.

a. I don't know where they were yesterday.

2. Она ничего не хочет.

b. I don't know. I never know anything.

3. Мы никого не любим.

c. She hasn't been anywhere yet.

4. Я не получил ни одного письма.

d. I am a foreigner. I know nothing about [in] this town.

5. Что это за книга?

6. Он давно хотел посмотреть этот балет.

e. Thanks a lot.

f. Tell me, please, where the post office is.

7. Я иностранец. Я ничего не знаю в этом городе.

g. I haven't received one letter.

8. Она ещё нигде не была.

h. She doesn't want anything.

9. Скажите, пожалуйста, где здесь почта?

i. What's playing at the theatre today?

10. Они никогда не говорят, куда они идут.

j. He has wanted to see this ballet for a long time.

11. Я не знаю, где они были вчера.

k. We don't love anyone.

12. Что сегодня идёт в театре?

l. What sort of book is this?

13. Я не знаю. Я никогда ничего не знаю.

m. He doesn't know anything.

14. Большое спасибо.

n. You have to go three stops.

15. Вам нужно проехать   o. They never say where they
    три остановки.   are going.

ANSWERS
1–m; 2–h; 3–k; 4–g; 5–l; 6–j; 7–d; 8–c; 9–f; 10–o; 11– a; 12–i;
13–b; 14–e; 15–n.

LESSON 24

A. Sample Sentences: Small Talk

Вчера́ бы́ло воскресе́нье.	Yesterday was Sunday.
Вчера́ никто́ не рабо́тал.	Yesterday no one was working.
Мы сиде́ли до́ма весь день.	We stayed home all day.
Ле́том на да́че бы́ло о́чень жа́рко.	It was very hot in the country during the summer.
Я был на ле́кции.	I was at the lecture.
Ле́ктор говори́л об Аме́рике.	The lecturer was talking about America.
Он сказа́л, что в Ю́жной Аме́рике говоря́т по-испа́нски и по-португа́льски.	He said that in South America they speak Spanish and Portuguese.
Я учи́л англи́йский язы́к, когда́ я был ещё ма́леньким ма́льчиком.	I studied English when I was still a small boy.
Толсто́й написа́л рома́н «Война́ и мир».	Tolstoi wrote the novel *War and Peace*.

Его́ жена́ ему́ всегда́ помога́ла.	His wife was always helping him.
Он мог рабо́тать по це́лым дням.	He could work for days at a time.
Она́ могла́ писа́ть мно́го часо́в в день.	She could write many hours a day.
Говоря́т, что она́ перепи́сывала э́тот рома́н де́сять раз.	They say that she copied this novel ten times.
Я уста́л.	I am tired.
Я устаю́, когда́ (я) мно́го говорю́.	I become tired when I talk a lot.
Он устава́л о́чень бы́стро.	He used to become tired very quickly.
Она́ опозда́ла.	She was late.
Она́ всегда́ опа́здывает.	She is always late.
Они́ шли домо́й, когда́ неожи́данно пошёл дождь.	They were walking home when it started to rain unexpectedly.
Дождь шёл це́лый день (весь день), всю неде́лю, весь ме́сяц.	It rained [rain fell] all day, all week, all month.
Машини́стка пришла́ на рабо́ту и начала́ печа́тать.	The typist arrived at the office and began to type.
Он игра́л. Она́ слу́шала. Он ко́нчил игра́ть.	He played. She listened. He finished playing.
Она́ заговори́ла.	She began to speak.
В час дня все пошли́ обе́дать.	At one o'clock everyone went to have lunch.

Я пообе́дал и верну́лся на рабо́ту.	I had lunch [lunched] and returned to the office.
Он был здесь не́сколько дней тому́ наза́д.	He was here several days ago.
Я прие́хал в Москву́ две неде́ли тому́ наза́д.	I came to Moscow two weeks ago.
Я ещё не получи́л ни одного́ письма́.	I still haven't received a single letter.
По́чта прихо́дит ра́но у́тром.	The mail comes early in the morning.
Она́ ду́мала, что здесь все говоря́т по-англи́йски.	She thought that everyone spoke English here.
Она́ купи́ла всё, что ей бы́ло ну́жно.	She bought every thing [all] that she needed.
Он купи́л мно́го нену́жных веще́й.	He bought a lot of unnecessary things.
Она́ люби́ла его́ когда́-то.	She loved him at one time.
И он люби́л её, но э́то бы́ло мно́го лет тому́ наза́д.	And he loved her, but that was many years ago.

B. VERBS: PERFECTIVE AND IMPERFECTIVE ASPECTS

Russian verbs can be perfective or imperfective. Imperfective verbs express continuous or repeated action. They have three tenses: past, present, and future.

Perfective verbs indicate completion of action, beginning of action, or both, and have only two tenses: past and future.

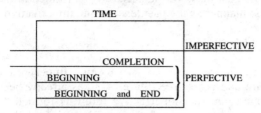

Some perfective verbs are formed by adding pre-fixes–such as с, на, вы, в, по–to imperfective verbs. When a prefix is added to a verb, the per-fective aspect of the verb is formed. Very often the meaning of the verb is changed at the same time.

IMPERFECTIVE	PERFECTIVE
писа́ть to write	написа́ть to write down
	переписа́ть to copy

When the meaning of the verb changes, the new verb переписа́ть, to copy, that has been formed must have its own imperfective. To form the imperfective of such new verbs, the suffix ыв or ив or ав is added:

IMPERFECTIVE	PERFECTIVE	IMPERFECTIVE
		перепи́сывать to copy
чита́ть to read	прочита́ть	прочи́тывать
	(to finish reading or to read through)	
	перечита́ть	перечи́тывать
		(to read over)
знать to know	узна́ть	узнава́ть
	(to find out or to recognize)	

The past tense of the perfective is formed in the same manner as the past tense of the imperfective.

C. THE FUTURE TENSE

The future tense has two forms: imperfective future and perfective future. As has already been pointed out, the imperfective future is formed by using the auxiliary verb **быть** with the infinitive of the imperfective verb.

я бу́ду	I will
ты бу́дешь	you will
он бу́дет говори́ть, чита́ть	he will speak, read,
мы бу́дем понима́ть, etc.	we will understand, etc.
вы бу́дете	you will
они́ бу́дут	they will

The perfective future is formed without using the auxiliary verb **быть**.

PRESENT		PERFECTIVE FUTURE	
я пишу́	I write	я напишу́	I will write
ты говори́шь	you speak	ты ска́жешь	you will say
он идёт	he goes	он придёт	he will come
мы чита́ем (it)	we read	мы прочита́ем	we will read
вы смо́трите	you look	вы посмо́трите	you will look
они́ е́дут come	they go [ride]	они́ прие́дут	they will [riding]

NOTICE

The perfective verb is conjugated in the future in the same way that the imperfective is conjugated in the present.

QUIZ 14

1. Лектор говорил об Америке.	a. He was in town.
2. Вчера я писал весь день.	b. I had lunch and returned to the office.
3. Она написала вчера два письма.	c. She, also, always says that.
4. Он сказал, что он ничего не знает.	d. At one o'clock everyone went to lunch.
5. Она тоже всегда это говорит.	e. She was home.
6. Она опоздала сегодня	f. She is always late.
7. Дождь шёл целый день.	g. Yesterday I wrote all day.
8. Она всегда опаздывает.	h. She was late today.
9. В час дня все пошли обедать.	i. He was in America many years ago.
10. Он купил много ненужных вещей.	j. He said that he knows nothing.
11. Я позавтракал и вернулся на работу.	k. We were in the office.
12. Она была дома.	l. The lecturer was talking about America.
13. Он был в городе.	m. She wrote two letters yesterday.
14. Мы были на работе.	n. It was raining all day.
15. Он был в Америке много лет тому назад.	o. He bought a lot of unnecessary things.

ANSWERS
1–l; 2–g; 3–m; 4–j; 5–c; 6–h; 7–n; 8–f; 9–d; 10–o; 11–b; 12–e; 13–a; 14–k; 15–i.

LESSON 25

A. MEETING A FRIEND IN MOSCOW

Здра́вствуйте,
  Никола́й Ива́нович!

Hello, Nikolai
  Ivanovich.

Здра́вствуйте,
  Наде́жда Петро́вна,
  как давно́ я вас не
  ви́дел!

Hello, Nadezhda
  Petrovna, I haven't
  seen you in a long
  time.

Вы давно́ в Москве́?

Have you been in
  Moscow long?

Нет. Я прие́хал
  неде́лю тому́ наза́д.

No. I arrived a week
  ago.

Где вы живёте?

Where are you staying
  [living]?

Я живу́ у бра́та.
  У него́ больша́я
  кварти́ра.

I'm staying [living]
  with my brother. He
  has a large apartment.

Ваш брат хорошо́
  говори́т
  по-англи́йски,
  пра́вда?

Your brother speaks
  English well, doesn't
  he? [isn't it true]?

Да. Он говори́т,
  пи́шет и чита́ет
  по-англи́йски.

Yes. He speaks,
  writes, and reads
  English.

Его́ жена́ амери-
  ка́нка, да?

His wife is an
  American, isn't she?

Да, вот почему́ он
  так хорошо́ зна́ет
  англи́йский язы́к.

Yes, that's why he
  knows English so well.

Скажи́те, а как его́
  жена́ говори́т
  по-ру́сски?

Tell me, how does his
  wife speak Russian?

Не о́чень хорошо́.

Not very well.

Она́ понима́ет почти́

She understands almost

всё, но говори́т пло́хо.	everything, but speaks little.
Вы давно́ зна́ете его́ жену́?	Have you known his wife for a long time?
Коне́чно. Я знал её ра́ньше моего́ бра́та.	Of course. I knew her before my brother did.
Говоря́т, что она́ о́чень ми́лая же́нщина.	They say that she's a very pleasant girl [woman].
Да, она́ у́мная, краси́вая и о́чень ми́лая.	Yes, she's intelligent, pretty, and very pleasant.
У них есть де́ти?	Do they have children?
Да, есть.	Yes, they have.
А как они́ говоря́т— по-ру́сски и́ли по-англи́йски?	What do they speak— Russian or English?
Де́ти говоря́т и по-ру́сски и по-англи́йски.	The children speak both Russian and English.
Как э́то хорошо́! Я ду́маю, что все де́ти должны́ знать хотя́ бы два языка́.	Isn't that good! I think that all children should know at least two languages.
Ну, коне́чно, все должны́ знать два языка́.	Well, of course everybody should know two languages.
Вот вы—ру́сский и о́чень хорошо́ говори́те по-англи́йски.	Here you're Russian, and you speak English very well.
А вы—америка́нка и о́чень хорошо́ говори́те по-ру́сски.	And you're an American and speak Russian very well.
Нет, ещё не о́чень хорошо́, но я всё	No, not very well yet, but I'm studying all

вре́мя занима́юсь и бу́ду хорошо́ говори́ть. по-ру́сски. Вы уви́дите.	the time and will speak Russian well. You'll see.
С кем вы занима́етесь?	With whom are you studying?
Ра́ньше у меня́ был о́чень хоро́ший учи́тель, но он уе́хал, потому́ что его́ мать заболе́ла. И тепе́рь я занима́юсь сама́.	I had a very good teacher before, but he went away because his mother became ill. And now I'm studying by myself.
Но вы зна́ете, э́то о́чень тру́дно.	But you know, that's very difficult.
Коне́чно, тру́дно занима́ться само́й, но я уже́ доста́точно мно́го прошла́, а чем бо́льше вы зна́ете, тем ле́гче продолжа́ть.	Of course it's difficult to study by oneself, but I've already gone through quite a lot, and the more you know, the easier it is to continue.

B. The Personal Pronouns: Сам, Себя́

The personal pronoun сам, сама́, само́, са́ми (by oneself) is declined like other personal pronouns (see table, Lesson 11). It modifies the agent of the sentence.

The reflexive pronoun себя́ (oneself) has no gender and no nominative form. It refers to the verb in that sentence.

Я занима́юсь сам.	I study by myself.
Я сказа́л ему́ самому́.	I told him [himself].

Само́ собо́й разуме́ется.	It goes without saying. [It reasons itself.]
Он разгова́ривает сам с собо́й.	He talks to himself [himself with himself].
Он никогда́ сам о себе́ ничего́ не говори́т.	He never says anything about himself.
Она́ взяла́ с собо́й мою́ кни́гу.	She took my book with her.
Она́ сама́ сши́ла себе́ пла́тье.	She made a dress for herself.

The verb жить (to live), although it ends on -ить, belongs to the first conjugation and is conjugated as follows:

я живу́	I live
ты живёшь	you live
он живёт	he lives
мы живём	we live
вы живёте	you live
они живу́т	they live

C. WORD STUDY

стро́ить-постро́ить	to build
внима́тельно	attentively
конча́ть-ко́нчить	to finish
па́мятник	monument
нау́чный	scholarly
обсужда́ть-обсуди́ть	to discuss
ме́сяц	month
всегда́	always
пока́	so long

QUIZ 15

1. Она русская и очень хорошо говорит по-английски.
2. Где вы живёте?
3. Скажите, как его жена говорит по-русски?
4. У них есть дети.
5. Вы давно знаете его?
6. Раньше у меня был очень хороший учитель.
7. Я всё время занимаюсь.
8. Мы будем хорошо говорить по-русски. Вы увидите.
9. Они приехали в Москву неделю тому назад.
10. Я занимаюсь сам.
11. Чем больше вы знаете, тем легче продолжать.
12. Он уехал, потому что его мать заболела.
13. Все должны знать хотя бы два языка.
14. С кем вы занимаетесь?
15. Я давно вас не видел.

a. I study all the time.
b. They have children.
c. The more you know, the easier it is to continue
d. I haven't seen you in a long time.
e. We will speak Russian well, you'll see.
f. With whom are you studying?
g. She is Russian and speaks English very well.
h. He went away because his mother became ill.
i. Where do you live?
j. Have you known him long?
k. Tell me, how does his wife speak Russian?
l. I had a very good teacher before.
m. They arrived in Moscow a week ago.
n. Everyone should know at least two languages.
o. I study by myself.

ANSWERS
1–g; 2–i; 3–k; 4–b; 5–j; 6–l; 7–a; 8– e; 9–m; 10–o; 11–c; 12–h; 13–n; 14–f; 15–d.

LESSON 26

A. Shopping: In a Store

Где здесь хоро́ший магази́н?	Where is there a good store here?
Како́й магази́н вам ну́жен?	What kind of a store do you need?
Мне ну́жно купи́ть бума́гу, карандаши́ и словари́.	I have to buy paper, pencils, and dictionaries.
Тако́й магази́н есть на Не́вском проспе́кте.	There's a store like that on Nevsky Prospect.
(В магази́не)	(In the store)
Есть у вас словари́?	Do you have dictionaries?
Коне́чно. Како́й слова́рь вам ну́жен?	Of course. What kind of dictionary do you need?
Я америка́нец, и как вы слы́шите, не совсе́м хорошо́ говорю́ по-ру́сски.	I'm an American, and, as you (can) hear, don't speak Russian too well.
Очеви́дно, вам нужны́ ру́сско-англи́йский и а́нгло-ру́сский словари́. Вот о́ба словаря́ в одно́м то́ме, а вот побо́льше, в двух тома́х.	Obviously you need Russian-English and English-Russian dictionaries. Here are both dictionaries in one volume, and this one a bit larger, in two volumes.
Ско́лько они́ сто́ят?	How much do they cost?
Однотомный три́дцать	The one-volume [dictio-

рубле́й, а двухто́мный семьдеся́т.	nary] thirty rubles, and the two-volume, seventy.
Как вы ду́маете, како́й из них лу́чше? Я не зна́ю.	What do you think– which of them is better? I don't know.
Это де́ло вку́са.	It's a question of taste.
Е́сли вы мно́го чита́ете и перево́дите, возьми́те большо́й.	If you read a lot and translate, take the big one.
Нет, мне ну́жен слова́рь то́лько для разгово́ра.	No, I need a dictionary only for conversation.
Ну, тогда́ возьми́те ма́ленький. Его́ удо́бно носи́ть с собо́й.	Well, then, take the little one. It's convenient to carry with you.
Скажи́те, пожа́луйста, а у вас есть карандаши́?	Tell me, please, do you have pencils?
Вот чёрные карандаши́, вот кра́сные и си́ние.	Here are black pencils; here are red and blue ones.
Э́ти твёрдые, а э́ти мя́гкие.	These are hard, and these are soft.
Покажи́те мне, пожа́луйста, авторучки.	Please show me (some) fountain pens.
Вот э́то о́чень хоро́шая ру́чка. Мы гаранти́руем, что она́ не бу́дет течь.	Here's a very good pen. We guarantee that it won't leak.
Ну, вот и хорошо́. Это, пожа́луй, всё.	That's good. I think that's all.
Да́йте мне двена́дцать карандаше́й, одну́	Give me a dozen pencils, one pen,

ру́чку и вот э́ту коро́бку пи́счей бума́ги.	and that box of writing paper there.
А слова́рь вы не возьмёте?	Aren't you going to take the dictionary?
Ах да! Коне́чно! Да́йте мне ма́ленький, одното́мный.	Oh yes! Of course! Give me the little one-volume (dictionary).
Ско́лько с меня́?	How much do I owe you?
Слова́рь три́дцать рубле́й, карандаши́ рубль два́дцать, ру́чка пять рубле́й и бума́га три рубля́– всего́ три́дцать де́вять рубле́й два́дцать копе́ек.	The dictionary is thirty rubles; the pencils, one ruble, twenty kopecks; the pen, five rubles; and the paper, three rubles–in all, thirty-nine rubles, twenty kopecks.
Пожа́луйста.	Here you are.
Спаси́бо. Всего́ хоро́шего.	Thank you. All the best.
До свида́ния.	Good-bye.
Заходи́те ещё.	Come again!

B. Perfective Verbs with Different Roots

IMPERFECTIVE	PERFECTIVE	IMPERFECTIVE
говори́ть to speak	сказа́ть to tell	
	заговори́ть to begin talking	загова́ривать
	рассказа́ть to tell a story	расска́зывать
	заказа́ть to order something	зака́зывать to be made or done
	приказа́ть to order, to command	прика́зывать

Prefixes can be added to either говори́ть or каза́ть, but each combination forms a new verb; e.g.:

за-говори́ть	to begin talking
за-каза́ть	to order something
от-говори́ть	to talk someone out of something
от-каза́ть	to refuse

The perfective of the verb брать (*to take*) is взять. It is conjugated as follows:

PRESENT TENSE		PERFECTIVE FUTURE	
брать		взять	
я беру́	I take	я возьму́	I will take
ты берёшь	you take	ты возьмёшь	you will take
он берёт	he takes	он возьмёт	he will take
мы берём	we take	мы возьмём	we will take
вы берёте	you take	вы возьмёте	you will take
они беру́т	they take	они возьму́т	they will take

QUIZ 16

1. Вот оба словаря в одном томе.
2. Как вы думаете, какой из них лучше?
3. Покажите мне, пожалуйста, авторучки.
4. Дайте мне двенадцать карандашей.
5. Как вы слышите, я не совсем хорошо говорю по-русски.
6. Мне нужен словарь только для разговора.
7. Я специально за этим пришёл.

a. These pencils are hard, and these are soft.
b. I need a dictionary only for conversation.
c. In all, thirty-nine rubles, twenty kopecks.
d. I came especially for that.
e. If you read and translate a lot, take the big one.
f. I need a bookstore.
g. Here are both dictionaries in volume.

8. Сколько они стоят?
9. Всего тридцать девять рублей двадцать копеек.
10. Очевидно, вам нужен большой хороший словарь.
11. Если вы много читаете и переводите, возьмите большой.
12. Эти карандаши, твёрдые, а эти мягкие.
13. Мне нужен книжный магазин.
14. Какой словарь вам нужен?
15. Всего хорошего. Заходите ещё.

h. Give me twelve pencils.
i. Please show me (some) fountain pens.
j. What do you think—which of them is better?
k. How much do they cost?
l. All the best. Come in again.
m. What kind of a dictionary do you need?
n. As you (can) hear, I don't speak Russian well.
o. Obviously you need a good, big dictionary.

ANSWERS

1–g; 2–j; 3–i; 4–h; 5–n; 6– b; 7–d; 8–k; 9– c; 10–o; 11–e; 12–a; 13–f; 14–m; 15–l.

LESSON 27

A. Verbs of Motion

Verbs of motion have many variations of meaning. A different verb is used to express movement by a conveyance than is used to express movement by foot.

Each of these verbs has two forms: i.e., one describes a single action in one direction; the other, a repeated action. All of these forms are imperfective. The perfective is formed by adding a prefix to a single-action verb. However, it must be emphasized that the addition of the prefix changes the meaning of the verb. The same prefix with the repeated-action verb forms the imperfective of the new verb.

Study the following chart.

Imperfective	Repeated Action		One Action	Perfective
	ходи́ть	to go on foot	идти́	
	е́здить	to go by vehicle	е́хать	
выходи́ть		to go out on foot		вы́йти
выезжа́ть		to go out by vehicle		вы́ехать
приходи́ть		to come on foot [arrive]		прийти́
приезжа́ть		to come by vehicle [arrive]		прие́хать
заходи́ть		to drop in [visit] on foot		зайти́
заезжа́ть		to drop in [visit] by vehicle		зае́хать
находи́ть		to find		найти́
	носи́ть	to carry on foot	нести́	
	вози́ть	to carry by vehicle	везти́	
приноси́ть		to bring on foot		принести́
привози́ть		to bring by vehicle		привезти́

Идти
to go on foot
(single action in one direction)

Present Tense	Past Tense
я иду́	
ты идёшь	
он идёт	он шёл
мы идём	она́ шла
вы идёте	оно́ шло
они́ иду́т	они́ шли

Ходи́ть
to go on foot
(repeated action)

Present Tense	Past Tense
я хожу́	Regular
ты хо́дишь	
он хо́дит	
мы хо́дим	
вы хо́дите	
они́ хо́дят	

Е́хать
to go by vehicle
(single action in one direction)

Present Tense	Past Tense
я е́ду	Regular
ты е́дешь	
он е́дет	
мы е́дем	
вы е́дете	
они́ е́дут	

Е́здить
to go by vehicle
(repeated action)

PRESENT TENSE	PAST TENSE
я е́зжу	Regular
ты е́здишь	
он е́здит	
мы е́здим	
вы е́здите	
они́ е́здят	

Нести́
to carry on foot
(single action in one direction)

PRESENT TENSE	PAST TENSE
я несу́	
ты несёшь	
он несёт	он нёс
мы несём	она несла́
вы несёте	оно несло́
они́ несу́т	мы несли́
	вы несли́
	они несли́

Носи́ть
to carry on foot
(repeated action)

PRESENT TENSE	PAST TENSE
я ношу́	Regular
ты но́сишь	
он но́сит	
мы но́сим	
вы но́сите	
они́ но́сят	

Везти́
to carry by vehicle
(single action in one direction)

PRESENT TENSE	PAST TENSE
я везу́	
ты везёшь	
он везёт	он вёз
мы везём	она́ везла́
вы везёте	оно́ везло́
они́ везу́т	они везли́

Вози́ть
to carry by vehicle
(repeated action)

PRESENT TENSE	PAST TENSE
я вожу́	Regular
ты во́зишь	
он во́зит	
мы во́зим	
вы во́зите	
они́ во́зят	

QUIZ 17

In this quiz, or exercise, try to fill in the blanks with the proper form of "going" verbs, on foot or by vehicle, in one direction or denoting repeated action. Think carefully before checking your answers.

1. Мы _____ сегодня из Чикаго в Нью-Йорк. — Today we came to New York from Chicago.

2. Я _____ в библиотеку каждый день. — I go to the library every day.

3. Сегодня он не _____ в библиотеку. — Today he is not going to the library.

4. Они _____ на дачу каждый год. — They go to the country every year.

5. В этом году они _____ к морю. — This year they are going to the seashore.

6. Я видел её сегодня, когда она _____ в школу. — I saw her today when she was going to school.

7. Она _____ с собой две книги. — She was carrying two books with her.

8. Наша школа очень далеко и мы должны _____ на автобусе. — Our school is very far, and we have to [must] go by bus.

ANSWERS
1. приехали; 2. хожу; 3. идёт; 4. ездят; 5. едут; 6. шла; 7. несла; 8. ездить.

B. In a Hotel

Здра́вствуйте. Мы то́лько что прие́хали из Нью-Йо́рка. — How do you do. We've just arrived from New York.

У вас есть свобо́дные ко́мнаты? — Do you have any vacant [free] rooms?

Да, есть. — Yes, we do (have).

На како́м этаже́ э́ти ко́мнаты? — What floor are these rooms on?

На пя́том. — On the fifth.

Эта комната слишком тёмная.	This room is too dark.
На девятом этаже есть комната, окна которой выходят на улицу.	On the ninth floor there is a room where the windows[the windows of which] face the street.
Можно посмотреть?	May I see it? [Is it possible to look?]
Да, пожалуйста.	Yes, please.
Эта комната мне очень нравится.	I like this room very much.
Пожалуйста, принесите мой багаж (мои вещи) сюда.	Please bring my baggage [my things] here.
Скажите, пожалуйста, есть ли здесь парикмахерская?	Tell me, please, is there a barbershop here?
Парикмахерская–на втором этаже.	The barbershop is on the second floor.
Она открыта с девяти часов утра до пяти часов вечера.	It's open from nine in the morning to five o'clock in the after- noon.
А на каком этаже портной?	And what floor is the tailor on?
Мне надо погладить костюм.	I have to have a suit pressed.
Портной на пятом этаже	The tailor is on the fifth floor.
Кому можно отдать бельё?	To whom should [may] I give my laundry?
Тут у меня несколько рубашек и нижнее бельё.	I have [here] several shirts and some underwear.

Вы мо́жете отда́ть ва́ше бельё де́вушке, кото́рая убира́ет ва́шу ко́мнату.	You may give your laundry to the girl who cleans your room.
Когда́ оно́ бу́дет гото́во?	When will it be ready?
Бельё обы́чно быва́ет гото́во че́рез два дня.	Laundry is usually ready in two days.
Э́то меня́ вполне́ устра́ивает.	That suits me completely.
А мо́жно заказа́ть за́втрак к себе́ в ко́мнату?	May I order break-fast in my room?
Коне́чно. На ка́ждом этаже́ есть своё обслу́живание.	Of course. Each floor has its own service.

C. Imperfective and Perfective Forms of "To Give"

Imperfective (present)	Perfective (future)
дава́ть	дать

я даю́	I give	я дам	I will give
ты даёшь	you give	ты дашь	you will give
он даёт	he gives	он даст	he will give
мы даём	we give	мы дади́м	we will give
вы даёте	you give	вы дади́те	you will give
они даю́т	they give	они даду́т	they will give

от-дава́ть	to give out, away	от-да́ть
пере-дава́ть	to pass	пере-да́ть
за-дава́ть	to assign	за-да́ть
с-дава́ть	to deal (cards)	с-дать

D. In My Apartment

В ко́мнате сто́ит стол и два сту́ла. На одно́й стене́ виси́т ка́рта го́рода, а на друго́й две карти́ны. До́ма у меня́ в кварти́ре две ко́мнаты: спа́льня и гости́ная. Гости́ная о́чень больша́я. В гости́ной три окна́ и все выхо́дят на у́лицу. В спа́льне то́лько одно́ окно́, и не на у́лицу. Поэ́тому в спа́льне о́чень ти́хо. В спа́льне стои́т больша́я крова́ть, комо́д и шкаф для оде́жды.

There are a table and two chairs in the room. A map of the city hangs on one wall, and two pictures on the other. I have a one-bedroom apartment [at home I have two rooms in my apartment]: a bedroom, and a living room. In the living room there are three windows, all of which face the street. There is only one window in the bedroom, and that does not face the street. Therefore the bedroom is very quiet. In the bedroom there is a large bed, a bureau, and a closet for clothes.

Ку́хня ма́ленькая, но о́чень удо́бная. В ней всё есть: и га́зовая плита́, и холоди́льник, и мно́го по́лок и я́щиков для посу́ды. На окне́ в ку́хне краси́вые ро́зовые занаве́ски.

The kitchen is small, but very comfortable. It is fully equipped with [there is all (the equipment)] a gas stove, a refrigerator, and a lot of shelves and drawers for dishes. There are pretty pink curtains on the kitchen window.

QUIZ 18

1. У вас есть свободные комнаты?	a. The barbershop is on the second floor.
2. Вы можете отдать ваше бельё сегодня и оно будет готово завтра.	b. Tell me, please, where the barbershop is.
3. Это меня вполне устраивает.	c. I have to have a suit pressed.
4. Окна этой комнаты выходят на улицу.	d. We've just arrived from New York.
5. Скажите, пожалуйста, где парикмахерская?	e. The office is open from nine in the morning to five in the afternoon.
6. Парикмахерская—на втором этаже.	f. The tailor is on the fifth floor.
7. Мы только что приехали из Нью-Йорка.	g. The windows of this room face the street.
8. Мне надо погладить костюм.	h. Do you have any vacant [free] rooms?
9. Портной на пятом этаже.	i. This suits me completely.
10. Контора открыта с девяти часов утра до пяти часов вечера.	j. You may give (out) your laundry today, and it will be ready tomorrow.

ANSWERS
1–h; 2–j; 3–i; 4–g; 5–b; 6–a; 7–d; 8–c; 9–f; 10–e.

LESSON 28

A. In a Restaurant

Максим:

Вот, здесь о́коло окна́ хоро́ший сто́лик.

Пётр:

Очень хорошо́. Я о́чень люблю́ смотре́ть в окно́.

Maxim:

Look, here's a good table near the window. Let's sit here.

Peter:

Very good. I like to look out the window.

Максим:

Дава́йте посмо́трим,
что сего́дня на обе́д.
Бара́нина жа́реная,
Бифште́кс
натура́льный
и́ли бифште́кс
ру́бленый. Бли́нчики
с мя́сом. Суп из
све́жих овоще́й.
Карто́фельное пюре́.

Maxim:

Let's see what they
have for dinner
today. Lamb chops,
regular steak or
chopped sirloin,
blinchiki with meat,
fresh vegetable soup,
mashed potatoes.

Пётр:

Зна́ете, что я возьму́?
Я хочу́ хоро́шей ры́бы.
Я о́чень люблю́ ры́бу,
и говоря́т, что здесь
её великоле́пно
гото́вят. На сла́дкое
я возьму́ компо́т из
сухофру́ктов.

Peter:

You know what I'll
take? I want some
good fish. I love
fish, and they say that
they prepare it very
well here. For dessert
I'll take a compote of
dried fruit.

Максим:

А я съем мясны́е
котле́ты и кисе́ль на
сла́дкое.

Maxim:

And I'll have meat
cutlets, and kissel for
dessert.

Пётр:

Официа́нт! Пожа́луйста
принеси́те нам
буты́лочку вина́.
Како́го-нибу́дь
хоро́шего кавка́зского.

Peter:

Waiter! Please bring
us a bottle of wine.
Some good Caucas-
ian wine.

Максим:

Ах, како́е
замеча́тельное вино́.
Ну, за ва́ше здоро́вье,
мой дорого́й друг!

Maxim:

Ah! What excellent
wine. Well, to your
health, my dear
friend!

Пётр:
**И за ва́ше то́же!
Тепе́рь ну́жно
закуси́ть. Вот
кусо́чек селёдки.
Е́шьте, пожа́луйста.
Ах, как вку́сно!**

Ма́ксим:
**Ну, ещё по бока́лу.
За мир, и за сча́стье
всех люде́й во всём
ми́ре.**

Пётр:
**Ну, зна́ете, за тако́й
тост нельзя́ не
вы́пить.**

Ма́ксим:
Ну, ещё оди́н бока́л?

Пётр:
**Нет, спаси́бо, я
бо́льше не хочу́.**

Ма́ксим:
Ну, ещё то́лько оди́н.

Пётр:
**Нет, я сказа́л уже́,
что бо́льше не хочу́,
и бо́льше пить
не бу́ду. Дава́йте есть.**

Ма́ксим:
**Ну, ничего́ с ва́ми не
поде́лаешь. Дава́йте
есть. А я вы́пил бы
ещё.**

Peter:
And to yours also!
Now we must eat a
bit. Here's a piece of
herring. Please have
some. Oh, how deli-
cious!

Maxim:
Let's each have
another glass. To
peace, and to the hap-
piness of all people in
the whole world.

Peter:
Well, you know, it's
impossible not to
drink to such a toast.

Maxim:
Well, another glass?

Peter:
No, thank you, I don't
want any more.

Maxim:
Just one more!

Peter:
No, I already said
that I don't want any
more and won't drink
any more. Let's eat.

Maxim:
Well, if I can't do
anything [nothing can
be done] with you...
Let's eat. But I would
have had another
[drunk another].

Пётр:	*Peter:*
Вы пейте, а я больше не хочу.	You drink, but I don't want any more.
Максим:	*Maxim:*
Официант! Сколько мы вам должны?	Waiter! How much do we owe you?

B. Foods and Utensils

масло	butter
хлеб	bread
соль	salt
перец	pepper
салат	salad, lettuce
подливка	sauce, gravy
зелень	green vegetables
овощи	vegetables
стакан воды	glass of water
чай	tea
кофе	coffee
фрукты	fruit
холодная закуска	hors d'oeuvres
второе блюдо	main course
сладкое	sweet course
десерт	dessert
нож	knife
столовая ложка	tablespoon or soup spoon
чайная ложечка	teaspoon
тарелка	dish
тарелочка	small dish
глубокая тарелка	soup bowl
блюдо	platter
чашка	cup
блюдце	saucer

стака́н	glass
салфе́тка	napkin
соло́нка	salt shaker

C. More: Use of Ещё or Бо́льше

The word "more" can be expressed in Russian by either ещё or бо́льше.

Вы хоти́те ещё ча́ю?	Do you want some more tea?
Нет, я бо́льше не хочу́.	No, I don't want any more.
Да, я хочу́ ещё.	Yes, I want (some) more.
Я приду́ к вам ещё раз.	I will come to you once more.
Я бо́льше к вам не приду́.	I will not come to you any more.

It is generally true that to express "more" affirmatively, еще is used; to say "no more" or "I don't want more," or when "more" is coupled with any negative verb, бо́льше is used.

Я хочу́ ещё.	I want more.
Он бо́льше не хо́чет.	He doesn't want more.
Я хочу́ ещё чита́ть.	I want to read some more.
Она́ вас бо́льше не лю́бит.	She doesn't love you any more.

D. CONJUGATION OF "To Eat"

есть	to eat
я ем	I eat
ты ешь	you eat
он ест	he eats
мы еди́м	we eat
вы еди́те	you eat
они едя́т	they eat

PAST TENSE

он ел	he	
она́ е́ла	she	ate
они́ е́ли	they	

QUIZ 19

1. Пожалуйста, принесите бутылочку вина.
2. Нет, я больше не хочу.

3. Нет, я ещё не кончил.
4. Я очень люблю рыбу.
5. Я ещё не ел рыбы в этом году.
6. Он больше не хочет мяса.

7. Почему вы больше не хотите?
8. Потому что я больше не голоден.
9. Я не ем, потому что я ещё не голоден.
10. На сладкое я возьму компот из сухофруктов.
11. Компота больше нет.

a. I can't eat any [thing] more.
b. He doesn't want any more meat.
c. Because I am not hungry any more.
d. There is no more compote.
e. Do you want anything else?
f. No, I don't want any more.
g. Please bring a bottle of wine.
h. I like fish very much.
i. I haven't eaten fish as yet this year.
j. No, thanks, I am finished.
k. No, I haven't finished yet.

12. Вы хотите ещё что-нибудь?	l. Too bad. As for me, I would have had another.
13. Нет, спасибо, я уже кончил.	m. For dessert I'll take compote of dried fruit.
14. Я больше ничего не могу съесть.	n. Why don't you want any more?
15. Жаль. А я бы выпил ещё.	o. I don't eat because I'm not hungry yet.

ANSWERS
1–g; 2–f; 3–k; 4–h; 5–i; 6–b; 7–n; 8–c; 9–o; 10–m; 11–d; 12–e; 13–j; 14–a.

LESSON 29

A. MORE ON PERFECTIVE AND IMPERFECTIVE VERBS

This lesson provides further examples of the use of perfective and imperfective verbs.

Мы бу́дем писа́ть пи́сьма.   писа́ть
We shall write letters.

Я напишу́ письмо́.   написа́ть
I shall start and finish the letter.

Я бу́ду опи́сывать всё.   опи́сывать
I shall describe everything [i.e., many things: imperfective].

Брат опи́шет вы́ставку.   описа́ть
(My) brother will describe the exhibition (completely).

Он встаёт ра́но ка́ждый   вставать
день.
He gets up early every day [imperfective].

Вчера́ он встал о́чень   встать
по́здно.
Yesterday he got up very late [once, completed:
perfective].

За́втра он вста́нет...   встать
Tomorrow he will get up [one time: perfective]...

Ле́том он бу́дет встава́ть...   встава́ть
During the summer he will get up [every day:
imperfective future]...

Я забы́л бума́жник до́ма.   забы́ть
I forgot my wallet at home [this one time: perfective past].

Он всегда́ всё забыва́ет.   забыва́ть
He always forgets everything [all the time: imper-
fective].

Он всё де́лает о́чень   де́лать
бы́стро.
He does everything very quickly [everything, all
the time: imperfective]

Он сде́лает э́то за́втра.   сде́лать
He will do this tomorrow [one time, tomorrow:
perfective future].

B. Sample Sentences: Daily Activities

Если за́втра бу́дет хоро́шая пого́да, я пойду́ гуля́ть в парк.	If the weather is good tomorrow, I will go to the park for a walk.
Ве́чером я бу́ду сиде́ть до́ма.	I'll stay home in the evening.
Мой брат бу́дет то́же до́ма за́втра.	My brother will also be home tomorrow.
Мы бу́дем писа́ть пи́сьма домо́й.	We'll write letters home.
Я напишу́ письмо́ в Нью-Йо́рк.	I'll write a letter to New York.
Брат напи́шет письмо́ сестре́ в Ме́ксику.	(My) brother will write a letter to (our) sister in Mexico.
Я бу́ду опи́сывать всё, что мы ви́дели в Москве́.	I'll describe everything we saw in Moscow.
Брат опи́шет худо́жественную вы́ставку.	(My) brother will describe the art exhibition.
За́втра у́тром мы пойдём в музе́й.	Tomorrow morning we'll go to the museum.
По доро́ге мы зайдём за мои́м това́рищем.	On the way we'll drop in to pick up my friend.
Он бу́дет нас ждать.	He'll wait for us.
Пусть подождёт. Я ждал его́ мно́го раз!	Let him wait. I've waited for him many times!
Я бы́стро помо́юсь, оде́нусь и причешу́сь.	I'll wash (myself), dress (myself), and comb my hair quickly.

Я всегда́ бы́стро мо́юсь, одева́юсь и причёсываюсь.	I always wash (myself), dress (myself), and comb my hair quickly.
Он встаёт ра́но ка́ждый день.	He gets up [rises] early every day.
Вчера́ он встал о́чень по́здно.	Yesterday he got up very late.
За́втра он вста́нет, как всегда́, ра́но.	Tomorrow he will get up early, as always.
Ле́том он бу́дет встава́ть в во́семь часо́в.	In the summer he will get up at eight o'clock.
Скажи́те ему́, что я бу́ду у него́ за́втра.	Tell him that I'll be at his house [by him] tomorrow.

C. More Verb Practice

Он всегда́ всё забыва́ет.	He always forgets everything.
По́езд отхо́дит в два часа́.	The train leaves at two o'clock.
Сего́дня он отойдёт в три часа́.	Today it will leave at three o'clock.
По́езд отошёл во́время.	The train left on time.
Вы говори́те сли́шком бы́стро. Я вас не понима́ю.	You talk too fast. I don't understand you.
Е́сли вы ска́жете всё э́то ме́дленно, я вас пойму́.	If you say all that slowly, I'll understand you.
Мы прочтём меню́ и пото́м зака́жем обе́д.	We'll read the menu and then order dinner.

Официа́нт ско́ро принесёт суп.	The waiter will bring the soup soon.
Я не могу́ бо́льше ждать.	I can't wait any longer.
Он смо́жет э́то сде́лать, е́сли полу́чит всё, что ему́ ну́жно.	He'll be able to do that if he gets everything he needs.

QUIZ 20

1. За́втра у́тром мы _____ в музе́й.
   Tomorrow morning we'll go to the museum.

2. Я всегда́ бы́стро _____.
   I always wash (myself) quickly.

3. Я бы́стро _____ и _____ в шко́лу.
   I'll wash (myself) quickly and go to school.

4. Он _____ ра́но ка́ждый день.
   He gets up early every day.

5. За́втра он _____, как всегда́, ра́но.
   Tomorrow he will get up early, as usual.

6. Ле́том он _____ во́семь часо́в.
   In the summer he will be getting up at eight o'clock.

7. Е́сли вы _____ всё э́то ме́дленно, я вас пойму́.
   If you will say all that slowly, I will (be able to) understand you.

8. Официа́нт ско́ро _____ суп.
   The waiter will bring the soup soon.

9. По́езд _____ во-вре́мя.
   The train left on time.

10. Я не могу́ _____ ждать.
    I can't wait any longer.

ANSWERS

1. пойдём; 2. мо́юсь; 3. помо́юсь, пойду́; 4. встаёт; 5. вста́нет; 6. бу́дет встава́ть; 7. ска́жете; 8. принесёт; 9. отошёл; 10. бо́льше.

LESSON 30

A. Introductions

Кто там?	Who is there?
Мо́жно войти́?	May one [I or we] come in?
Входи́те, пожа́луйста.	Please come in.
Позво́льте вам предста́вить моего́ дру́га.	Allow me to introduce my friend to you.
О́чень рад с ва́ми познако́миться.	I'm very glad to meet you [to become acquainted with you].
О́чень прия́тно.	Delighted. [Very pleasant.]
Разреши́те предста́виться.	Permit me to introduce myself.
Меня́ зову́т Ива́н Петро́вич Крыло́в.	My name is [they call me] Ivan Petrovich Krilov.
Сади́тесь, пожа́луйста.	Please have a seat.
Мо́жно вам предложи́ть ча́ю?	May I offer you some tea?
Вы хоти́те со мной поговори́ть?	You want to talk with me?
Что вам ну́жно?	What do you need?

B. At the Train Station

Скажи́те мне, пожа́луйста, где вокза́л?	Please tell me where the train station is.
Иди́те пря́мо до угла́, пото́м нале́во оди́н	Go straight to the corner, then one block to

кварта́л.	the left.
Где продаю́т биле́ты?	Where do they sell tickets?
Вон там ка́сса.	There's the ticket office.
Бо́же мой! Кака́я больша́я о́чередь!	Good heavens! What a long line [turn]!
Не беспоко́йтесь.	Don't worry.
О́чередь идёт о́чень бы́стро.	It moves quickly.
Да́йте мне, пожа́луйста, биле́т в Я́сную Поля́ну.	Please give me a ticket to Yasnaya Polyana.
Вам в одну́ сто́рону и́ли туда́ и обра́тно?	Do you want a one-way ticket or a round trip?
Туда́ и обра́тно, пожа́луйста.	Round trip, please.
Когда́ отхо́дит по́езд? Да́йте мне, пожа́луйста, расписа́ние поездо́в.	When does the train leave? Give me a timetable, please.
Поезда́ в Я́сную Поля́ну отхо́дят ка́ждый час.	Trains to Yasnaya Polyana leave every hour.
Где аэропо́рт?	Where is the airport?
Аэропо́рт о́чень далеко́.	The airport is very far away.
Туда́ ну́жно е́хать и́ли авто́бусом, и́ли на такси́.	You have to take a bus or a taxi to get there.
Вот э́ти такси́ е́дут то́лько в аэропо́рт.	[Here] these taxis go only to the airport.
Туда́ по кра́йней ме́ре по́лчаса езды́.	It's at least a half-hour trip.
В аэропорту́, пре́жде чем сесть на самолёт, ну́жно получи́ть	At the airport you have to get a boarding pass before you can get on

поса́дочный тало́н.	the plane.
Пойдёмте! Уже́ о́чень по́здно.	Let's go. It's very late already.
Я не люблю́ опа́здывать.	I don't like to be late.
Это такси́ свобо́дно?	Taxi, are you free?
Нам ну́жно в аэропо́рт.	We have to go to the airport.
Сади́тесь, пожа́луйста!	Get in, please.

C. IN CASE OF ILLNESS

Есть ли здесь в гости́нице до́ктор?	Is there a doctor in the hotel?
У меня́ о́чень боли́т голова́ и го́рло.	I have a headache and a sore throat.
У меня́ на́сморк.	I have a cold.
У меня́ боля́т зу́бы.	I have a toothache.
У него́ боли́т спина́.	His back hurts.
У неё температу́ра (жар).	She has a fever.
Нет ли у вас слаби́тельного?	Do you have a laxative?
Я о́чень пло́хо сплю.	I sleep very poorly.
Глаза́, у́ши, го́рло, нос, грудь, бок, ру́ки, но́ги; па́льцы на рука́х, па́льцы на нога́х.	Eyes, ears, throat, nose, chest (breast), side, hands, feet; fingers, toes.
Голова́ кру́жится.	I am dizzy [my head is spinning].
У вас температу́ра (жар).	You have a fever.
Боли́т живо́т.	My stomach aches.
Боль в желу́дке.	A pain in the stomach.
Мне ну́жно лежа́ть в посте́ли?	Do I have to stay in bed?

Да, обязáтельно.	Yes, definitely.
Меня тошни́т.	I am nauseous.
Принимáйте э́то лекáрство четы́ре рáза в день по столóвой ложке.	Take a tablespoon of this medicine four times a day.
Нá ночь сдéлайте себé согревáющий компрéсс.	At night apply a hot compress.
Ну́жно ли полоскáть гóрло, дóктор?	Should I gargle, doctor?
Да. Возьми́те одну́ чáйную лóжку сóли на стакáн горя́чей воды́ и полощи́те по крáйней мéре три рáза в день: кáждые четы́ре часá.	Yes. Take one teaspoon of salt to a glass of hot water and gargle at least three times a day, every four hours.
Не выходи́те, покá у вас не бу́дет нормáльная температу́ра.	Don't go out until your temperature is normal.

QUIZ 21

1. Можно вам предложить чаю?
2. Меня зовут Иван Крылов.
3. Скажите мне, пожалуйста, где вокзал?
4. Боже мой! Какая большая очередь!
5. Иван Крылов хорошо знает город.
6. Вам в одну сторону или туда и обратно?

a. Ivan Krilov knows the city well.
b. I don't like to be late.
c. Do you want a one-way or a round trip (ticket)?
d. May I offer you some tea?
e. My name is Ivan Krilov.
f. It's at least a half-hour trip.

7. Поезда отходят каждый час.

8. Туда по крайней мере полчаса езды.

9. Я не люблю опаздывать.

10. Не беспокойтесь, очередь идет очень быстро.

g. Don't worry. It moves [the sale goes] quickly.

h. Please tell me where the railroad station is.

i. Trains leave every hour.

j. Good heavens! What a long line!

ANSWERS
1–d; 2–e; 3–h; 4–j; 5–a; 6–c; 7–i; 8–f; 9–b; 10–g.

LESSON 31

A. MOSCOW THEATRES

Иван:

Если бы я знал, что сегодня идёт в московских театрах, я бы пошел в театр.

Ivan:

If I knew what's playing in the Moscow theatres today, I would go to the theatre.

Вера:

Есть такая маленькая книжечка, которая называется «Репертуар московских театров».

Vera:

There is a small book called *Program [Repertoire] of the Moscow Theatres.*

Иван:

Где её можно купить?

Ivan:

Where can one buy it?

Вера:

Во всех книжных киосках.

Vera:

At all book stands.

Иван:

Если бы я знал это раньше, то давно бы купил её.

Ivan:

If I had known that before [earlier], I would have bought it a long time ago.

Вера:

Ну, вот вИдите. Всё
    узнаётся в своё
    врЕмя.

Vera:

There, you see. In
    time one learns every-
    thing.

Иван:

МнОго теАтров в
    МосквЕ?

Ivan:

Are there many the-
    atres in Moscow?

Вера:

Да! Очень мнОго!
    ДавАйте посмОтрим.
    Вот БольшОй теАтр.
    Там идУт Оперы и
    балЕт.

Vera:

Yes. Very many. Let's
    look (at the book).
    Here is the Bolshoi
    Theatre. Operas and
    ballet play there.

Иван:

Где он нахОдится?

Ivan:

Where is it?

Вера:

На ТеатрАльной
    плОщади. ПотОм
    есть ФилиАл Боль-
    шОго теАтра, на
    ПУшкинской улице.
    Это тОже Оперный
    теАтр.

Vera:

On Theatre Square.
    Then there's an affili-
    ate of the Bolshoi
    Theatre on Pushkin
    Street. This is also an
    opera theatre.

Иван:

А где нахОдится
    МоскОвский
    ХудОжественный
    теАтр?

Ivan:

And where is the
    Moscow Art Theatre?

Вера:

На ПроЕзде
    ХудОжественного
    теАтра. Там идУт
    тОлько дрАмы и
    комЕдии. ПотОм есть
    МАлый теАтр, ТеАтр
    Имени ВахтАнгова,

Vera:

On Art Theatre Lane.
    Only dramas and
    comedies play there.
    Then there's the
    Maliy Theatre, the
    theatre named after
    Vahktangov, the

Теа́тр Опере́тты и т.д., и т.д.	Theatre of Operetta, etc., etc.
Ива́н:	*Ivan:*
А цирк есть в Москве́?	Is there a circus in Moscow?
Ве́ра:	*Vera:*
Ещё бы! Коне́чно есть. И како́й ещё замеча́тельный! Обяза́тельно пойди́те в цирк. Ста́рый цирк нахо́дится на Цветно́м Бульва́ре, дом 13. А но́вое зда́ние ци́рка на проспе́кте Верна́дского. А мо́жно ли доста́ть биле́ты на сего́дня, я не зна́ю. Ну́жно позвони́ть им по телефо́ну. Вот их но́мер: 212-16-40.	And how! Of course there is! And what an excellent one! Go to the circus without fail. The old circus is on Flower Boulevard, No. 13. But the new circus building is on Vernadsky Prospect. I don't know if it's possible to get tickets for today. You should (it is necessary to) call them (on the telephone). Here's their number: 212-16-40.
Ива́н:	*Ivan:*
Алло́, алло́. Скажи́те, пожа́луйста, есть биле́ты на сего́дня? Нет? Почему́? Ах, у вас сего́дня выходно́й. Как жаль... Сего́дня нет представле́ния. Ну, вот ви́дите как мне везёт.	Hello, hello. Do you have tickets for today? No? Why? Oh, you're closed today [today is your day off]. What a pity... There's no performance today. There, you see; that's my luck.

Вера:
Вы мóжете пойти́ зáвтра.

Vera:
You can go tomorrow.

Иван:
Нет, я ужé не успéю.

Ivan:
No, I won't have time.

Вера:
Почемý? Рáзве вы скóро уезжáете?

Vera:
Why? Are you leaving soon?

Иван:
Конéчно. Зáвтра. Ах, éсли бы я знáл об э́том рáньше, éсли бы мне сказáли э́то хотя́ бы недéлю томý назáд.

Ivan:
Of course. Tomorrow. Ah, if I had known about this earlier, if someone had told me that at least a week ago!

Вера:
Éсли бы я знáла, что вы ничегó не знáете, я бы сказáла вам.

Vera:
If I had known that you don't know anything, I would have told you.

Иван:
Вы же знáете, что я иностра́нец! Откýда же мне знать?

Ivan:
But you know that I'm a foreigner. How am I to know?

Вера:
Ну, прости́те! Ну, не серди́тесь!

Vera:
Oh, well, forgive me. Now, don't be angry.

Иван:
Я не сержýсь. Но мне всё же óчень, óчень жаль, что я не побывáл в ци́рке. Я так люблю́ цирк.

Ivan:
I'm not angry. But all the same I'm very, very sorry that I didn't get to the circus. I just love the circus.

Вера: *Vera:*
Ну, ничего́. В   Well, never mind.
  сле́дующий раз.   Next time.

B. Subjunctive and Conditional Moods

The formation of the conditional and subjunctive is likely to be among the most difficult grammatical constructions in any language. However, in Russian, it is one of the easiest. All you have to know is the particle **бы,** and that the past tense of the verb is used after it.

е́сли бы	if
Если бы я знал,	If I knew,
	Had I known,
я пошёл бы.	I would have gone.
	I would go.
Я позвони́л бы,	I would have called you,
е́сли бы у меня́ был	if I had your telephone
(бы) ваш телефо́н.	number.

C. Word Study

просто́й	simple
взро́слый	adult
гость	guest
рубль	ruble
назва́ние	title
пригла́шать-пригласи́ть	to invite
не́сколько	several
открыва́ть-откры́ть	to open
у́жин	supper
у́тро	morning

QUIZ 22

1. Ну, вот ви́дите. Всё узнаётся в своё вре́мя.
2. Почему́? Ра́зве вы ско́ро уезжа́ете?
3. Сего́дня нет представле́ния.
4. Если бы я знал э́то ра́ньше, то давно́ бы купи́л её.
5. Очень много. Давайте посмотрим.
6. Он очень хорошо говорит по-русски.
7. В нашем городе есть замечательный цирк.
8. Где он находится?
9. Я очень люблю цирк и хожу туда очень часто.
10. Моя сестра живет и работает в маленьком городе.
11. Два дня тому назад я был в театре.
12. В Московском художественном театре идут драмы и комедии.
13. А много театров в Москве?
14. Он никогда ничего не знает.
15. Она не знала, что сегодня этот магазин закрыт.
16. Скажите, пожалуйста, можно получить билеты на сегодня?
17. Ну, вот видите, как мне везет.
18. Вы можете пойти завтра.

a. He speaks Russian very well.
b. Are there many theatres in Moscow?
c. Where is it located?
d. I really love the circus and go there often.
e. I was in the theatre two days ago.
f. He never knows anything.
g. Tell me, please, is it possible to get tickets for today?
h. There, you see; that's my luck.
i. There's no performance today.
j. Oh, well, forgive me. Now, don't be annoyed.
k. There, you see. In time one learns everything.
l. Very many. Let's take a look.
m. She didn't know that this store is closed today.
n. We have an excellent circus in our town.
o. If I had known that before [earlier], I would have bought it a long time ago.
p. You can go tomorrow.
q. In the Moscow Art Theatre play dramas and comedies.
r. My sister lives and works in a small town.

19. Ну, простите! Ну, не сердитесь.	s. Well, never mind. Next time.
20. Ну, ничего. В следующий раз.	t. Why? Are you leaving soon?

NOTICE

Quizzes from this point on will include review sentences from previous lessons.

ANSWERS

1–k; 2–t; 3–i; 4–o; 5–l; 6–a; 7–n; 8–c; 9–d; 10–r; 11–e; 12–q; 13–b; 14–f; 15–m; 16–g; 17–h; 18–p; 19–j; 20–s.

LESSON 32

A. Useful Words & Expressions

Вот как!	Is that so!
Как бы не так!	Nothing of the sort!
Будьте как дома!	Make yourself at home.
как видно	as can be seen
Это как раз то, что мне нужно.	That's just what I need.
Это дело вкуса.	That's a matter of taste.
Совершенно верно.	Quite right. [Absolutely.]
Ещё бы.	And how! You bet!
кое-как	anyhow; haphazardly
Он холостой.	He's a bachelor.
Он женится.	He is getting married.
Он женат.	He is married.
Она ещё не замужем.	She is still not married.
Она выходит замуж.	She is getting married.
Она замужем.	She is married.
родной брат	brother

родна́я сестра́	sister
двою́родный брат	cousin (*m.*)
двою́родная сестра́	cousin (*f.*)
смотре́ть в о́ба	keep one's eyes open; be on one's guard
Э́тому не помо́жешь.	It can't be helped.
пока́ что	in the meantime
Поговори́те с ним, пока́ он там.	Talk to [with] him while he is there.
Оста́вьте меня́ в поко́е.	Leave me alone [in peace].
Он про́сто ничего́ не зна́ет.	He simply knows nothing.
Он ничего́ не име́ет про́тив э́того.	He has nothing against it. He doesn't mind.
Она́ лю́бит пуска́ть пыль в глаза́.	She likes to show off [to put on airs].
Тру́дно рабо́тать на пусто́й желу́док.	It's difficult to work on an empty stomach.
Нам с ва́ми по пути́.	We're going your way.
У вас золото́е се́рдце.	You have a heart of gold.
Благодарю́ вас от всего́ се́рдца.	Thank you from the bottom of my heart.
С глаз доло́й, из се́рдца вон.	Out of sight, out of mind.
бежа́ть изо все́х сил	to run as fast as one can
крича́ть изо все́х сил } крича́ть во всё го́рло	to scream at the top of one's voice
Он де́лает э́то по привы́чке.	He does it out of habit.
ле́гче сказа́ть, чем сде́лать	easier said than done
ска́зано–сде́лано	no sooner said than done
в ско́ром вре́мени	before long
ско́рая по́мощь	first aid

одни́м сло́вом	in a word; in short
други́ми слова́ми	in other words
Всё бу́дет забы́то.	Everything will be forgotten.
гла́вным о́бразом	mainly
таки́м о́бразом	in this way
на вся́кий слу́чай	just in case
во вся́ком слу́чае	in any case
в тако́м слу́чае	in this case

B. TELEPHONE CALLS

Отку́да мо́жно позвони́ть?	Where can I make a phone call?
Здесь есть телефо́нная бу́дка?	Is there a phone booth here?
Здесь есть телефо́нный спра́вочник?	Is there a telephone directory?
Опера́тор...	Operator...
Я хочу́ позвони́ть по э́тому но́меру.	I'd like to call this number.
Я хочу́ позвони́ть в Соединённые Шта́ты.	I'd like to call the United States.
Алло́.	Hello.
Говори́т...	This is...
Кто звони́т?	Who is calling?
С ке́м я говорю́?	To whom am I speaking?
Говори́те ме́дленно, пожа́луйста.	Speak slowly, please.
Э́то Андре́й.	This is Andrei.
Мо́жно поговори́ть с Вади́мом?	May I speak with Vadim?
Мой но́мер...	My number is...
Как мне связа́ться с опера́тором?	How do I get the operator?

Меня́ разъедини́ли. — I was cut off.

Вы могли́ бы соеди-
ни́ть меня́ ещё раз? — Could you connect me
again?

Я хоте́л бы
поговори́ть с... — I'd like to speak to...

Скажи́те ему́,
пожа́луйста, что я
звони́л. — Please tell him
I called.

C. WORD STUDY

забыва́ть-забы́ть	to forget
пра́здник	holiday
оши́бка	mistake
хо́лодно	cold (adv.)
гру́стный	sad
прекра́сный	wonderful
хлеб	bread
остано́вка	stop
дверь	door

LESSON 33

A. MORE VERBS OF MOTION

Ходи́ть из одно́й
ко́мнаты в другу́ю. — Walk from one room
to another.

Е́здить из го́рода
в го́род. — Travel from city to
city.

Он хо́дит в
библиоте́ку
о́чень ча́сто. — He goes [walks] to
the library very often.

Сего́дня мы идём
в теа́тр. — Today we are going
to the theatre.

Я всегда беру с собой бинокль; я очень близорукий.	I always take my binoculars with me; I'm very nearsighted.
Мне не нужен бинокль. Я дальнозоркий.	I don't need binoculars. I'm farsighted.
Он взял книгу и ушёл.	He took the book and went away.
Мой товарищ приехал вчера в Петербург.	My friend arrived in Petersburg yesterday.
Он ездит туда каждое лето.	He goes there every summer.
Я уезжаю завтра.	I'm going away tomorrow.
Я уеду завтра.	I'll go away tomorrow.
Я приеду во Владивосток только через восемь дней.	I'll get to [arrive in] Vladivostok in only eight days.
Сколько времени вы там будете?	How long [how much time] will you be there?
Я думаю, что пробуду там около двух недель.	I think that I'll spend about two weeks there.
Я уже был один раз во Владивостоке, но только проездом по дороге в Америку.	I've already been in Vladivostok once, but only (when) passing through on the way to America.
Я прилетел из Сан-Франциско.	I flew from San Francisco.
Я хотел бы поехать в Калифорнию.	I would like to go to California.
Говорят, что там замечательная природа.	They say that the scenery [nature] there is magnificent.

Почему́ же вы не е́дете?	Well, why don't you go?
У меня́ о́чень ма́ло свобо́дного вре́мени.	I have very little free time.
Вы мо́жете вы́ехать в нача́ле мая и провести́ там весь ию́нь.	You can leave at the beginning of May and spend all of June there.
Но я до́лжен прие́хать обра́тно в Росси́ю в конце́ ию́ня.	But I have to be back in Russia by the end of June.
Не бо́йтесь, вы успе́ете.	Don't be afraid. You'll make it.
Самолётом мо́жно путеше́ствовать о́чень бы́стро.	You can travel by plane very quickly.
Мо́жет быть, вы пра́вы. Попыта́юсь так и сде́лать.	Perhaps you're right. I'll try to arrange it.

QUIZ 23

1. Бу́дьте как дома.	a. He goes there every summer.
2. Сего́дня мы идём в теа́тр.	b. Everything will be forgotten.
3. Он взял кни́гу и ушёл	c. Where can I make a phone call?
4. Он е́здит туда́ ка́ждое ле́то.	d. Easier said than done.
5. Ско́лько вре́мени вы бу́дете там?	e. I'll try to arrange it.
6. Всё бу́дет забы́то.	f. You can leave at the beginning of May.
7. У меня́ о́чень ма́ло свобо́дного вре́мени.	g. Make yourself at home.
8. Я был там по доро́ге домо́й.	h. Don't be afraid; you'll make it [you'll have time].
9. Говоря́т, что там	i. He has to be back in town

замечательная природа.   by the end of June.

10. Откуда можно   j. He took the book and went
позвонить?   away.

11. Совершенно верно.   k. Today we are going to the
theatre.

12. Легче сказать, чем   l. How long will you be
сделать.   there?

13. Может быть, вы правы.   m. I have very little free
time.

14. Попытаюсь так и   n. She always takes her sister
сделать.   with her.

15. Он должен приехать   o. Leave me alone.
обратно в город в
конце июня.

16. Вы можете выехать   p. May I speak with Vadim?
в начале мая.

17. Не бойтесь, вы успеете.   q. Perhaps you're right.

18. Она всегда берёт с   r. Quite right.
собой свою сестру.

19. Можно поговорить   s. They say that the scenery
с Вадимом?   [nature] there is magnificent.

20. Оставьте меня в покое.   t. I passed [was] there on my
way home.

ANSWERS

1–g; 2–k; 3–j; 4–a; 5–l; 6–b; 7–m; 8–t; 9–s; 10–c; 11–r; 12–d;
13–q; 14–e; 15–i; 16–f; 17–h; 18–n; 19–p; 20–o.

LESSON 34

A. NEWSPAPERS, BOOKS, RADIO AND TELEVISION

Я хочу́ купи́ть газе́ту.   I'd like to buy a
newspaper.

Я хочу́ купи́ть журна́л.   I'd like to buy a
magazine.

У вас есть кни́ги на   Do you have any
англи́йском языке́?   books in English?

Есть музыкáльная прогрáмма?	Is there a music station?
Есть прогрáмма новостéй?	Is there a news station?
Есть прогрáмма прогнóза погóды?	Is there a weather station?
Во скóлько начáло передáчи?	What time is the program?
У вас есть телевизиóнная прогрáмма?	Do you have a television guide?
Во скóлько прогнóз погóды?	When is the weather forecast?
По какóму канáлу идёт передáча?	What channel is it on?

B. AT THE POST OFFICE

Я ищý Главпочтáмт.	I'm looking for the main post office.
Где нахóдится ближáйший почтóвый ящик?	Where's the nearest mailbox?
Скóлько стóит отпрáвить письмó в США?	How much is it for a letter to the U.S.?
открытка	postcard
Я хочý купить мáрки.	I would like to buy stamps.
Я хочý послáть эту посылку в США.	I would like to send this package to the United States.
Мóжно послáть телегрáмму в Нью-Йорк?	May I send a telegram to New York?
Скóлько стóит однó	How much is it per

сло́во?	word?
Придёт ли она́ за́втра у́тром?	Will it arrive tomorrow morning?
Како́е окно́ для телегра́мм?	Which window is it for telegrams?

C. Meeting An Old Friend

Я е́хал из Петербу́рга в Москву́. По доро́ге по́езд останови́лся в Но́вгороде. Но́вгород не о́чень большо́й го́род, но тут есть прекра́сный вокза́л и очень хоро́ший рестора́н. По́езд стои́т здесь це́лый час. Я вы́шел из по́езда и пошёл погуля́ть по платфо́рме, а пото́м реши́л пойти́ в рестора́н пое́сть. Как то́лько я вошёл в рестора́н, я встре́тил мою́ знако́мую из Москвы́.

I was on my way from Petersburg to Moscow. On the way, the train stopped in Novgorod. Novgorod is not a very large city, but there is an excellent station there and a very good restaurant. The train was to be there for a whole hour. I got off the train and went to stroll on the platform and then decided to go into the restaurant to eat. As soon as I walked into the restaurant, I met my friend from Moscow.

Серге́й:	*Sergei:*
Ве́ра Петро́вна, здра́вствуйте! Како́е интере́сное совпаде́ние!	Hello, Vera Petrovna! What an interesting coincidence.
Ве́ра:	*Vera:*
А! Серге́й Никола́евич! Как я ра́да вас ви́деть!	Ah, Sergei Nicholaevich! How glad I am to see you!

Сергей:
Что вы здесь де́лаете?
  Куда́ вы е́дете?

Sergei:
What are you doing
  here? Where are you
  going?

Вера:
Я е́ду в Приба́лтику.
  У меня́ о́тпуск.

Vera:
I'm going to the
  Baltics. I'm on
  vacation.

Сергей:
Вы полу́чите большо́е
удово́льствие.

Sergei:
You'll enjoy yourself
  greatly [receive great
  pleasure].

Приба́лтика прекра́сна.

The Baltic area is
  magnificent.

Вера:
Да, я зна́ю. Я так
  мно́го слы́шала и
  так мно́го чита́ла о
  мо́ре и сосно́вых
  леса́х. Я просто не
  могу́ дожда́ться
  той мину́ты, когда́
  передо мно́й бу́дет
  мо́ре.

Vera:
Yes, I know. I've
  heard so much and
  read so much about
  the ocean and pine
  forests. I simply
  can't wait for the
  moment when I'll
  see the ocean before
  me.

Сергей:
Ну тепе́рь уже́ не
  до́лго ждать. От
  Но́вгорода о́чень
  бли́зко. Давно́ вы
  из Москвы́?.

Sergei:
Well, now you won't
  have to wait long.
  It's very close to
  Novgorod. Are you
  away from Moscow
  very long?

Вера:
Нет, то́лько три дня.
  Я вы́ехала в суббо́ту
  у́тром.

Vera:
No, only three days.
  I left Saturday morn-
  ing.

Сергей:
**Вы ви́дели моего́
бра́та пе́ред отъе́здом?**

Sergei:
Did you see my
brother before
leaving?

Вера:
**Да, коне́чно, я зашла́
к нему́ в четве́рг
ве́чером, но его́ не́
бы́ло до́ма.**

Vera:
Yes, of course, I
dropped in on him
Thursday evening,
but he wasn't home.

Сергей:
**Зна́чит вы его́ не
ви́дели?**

Sergei:
So [that means] you
didn't see him?

Вера:
**Нет, почему́ же. Я
оста́вила ему́ запи́ску,
и он позвони́л мне на
сле́дующий день и
пото́м пришёл ко мне.**

Vera:
No, why? I left him
a note, and he called
me the next day and
then came to see me.

Сергей:
**Как там всё в Москве́?
Всё в поря́дке?**

Sergei:
How's everything in
Moscow? Everything
all right?

Вера:
**Всё норма́льно. Жена́
ва́шего бра́та была́
больна́, но она́ уже́
попра́вилась и
чу́вствует себя́ непло́хо.**

Vera:
Everything's fine.
Your brother's wife
was sick, but she has
recovered and feels
quite well.

Сергей:
**Да, я зна́ю. Брат мне
писа́л, и я о́чень
волнова́лся.**

Sergei:
Yes, I know. My
brother wrote me,
and I was very
worried.

Вера:
**Когда́ вы прие́дете в
Москву́, пожа́луйста,**

Vera:
When you arrive in
Moscow, please call

позвони́те ма́ме и
скажи́те, что встре́тили
меня́. Вот она́
удиви́тся! Серге́й
Никола́евич, а
вы уже́ обе́дали?

Серге́й:

Нет, коне́чно нет,
пойдёмте вме́сте и
переку́сим.

Ве́ра:

Вот хорошо́, а то я
про́сто умира́ю с
го́лоду.

Серге́й:

Вот здесь свобо́дный
сто́лик. Дава́йте ся́дем
здесь. Когда́ вы
бу́дете в Ри́ге, не
забу́дьте подня́ться
на Порохову́ю Ба́шню.

Ве́ра:

Говоря́т, что э́то о́чень
интере́сно, э́то о́чень
ста́рое зда́ние. Пра́вда?

Серге́й:

Соверше́нно ве́рно. И
вы зна́ете, отту́да
открыва́ется
изуми́тельный вид на
весь го́род.

Ве́ра:

Мне да́же не ве́рится,

my mother and say
that you ran into me.
She'll be so sur-
prised. Sergei
Nicholaevich,
have you already
eaten?

Sergei:

No, of course not.
Let's go together and
have a bite.

Vera:

That's good, I'm sim-
ply dying of hunger.

Sergei:

Here's an empty
table. Let's sit here.
When you're in Riga,
don't forget to go up
to the top of the
fortress tower.

Vera:

They say that it's
[this is] very
interesting. It is a
very old building,
right?

Sergei:

Quite right. And you
know, from there,
there is [opens out]
an amazing view of
the whole city.

Vera:

I can hardly believe

что я всё это уви́жу.   [even don't believe]
                              that I will see all
                              this.

За обе́дом я рассказа́л Ве́ре Петро́вне всё,
что я знал о Приба́лтике: куда́ лу́чше всего
пойти́, что посмотре́ть, где мо́жно хорошо́
пое́сть. Час прошёл о́чень бы́стро, и я чуть
не опозда́л на свой по́езд. Я вскочи́л в по́езд
уже́ по́сле тре́тьего звонка́.

At dinner I told Vera Petrovna all that I knew
about the Baltics: where it's best to go, what to
see, and the best places to eat. The hour passed
very quickly, and I was almost late for my train. I
jumped on the train after the third bell had already
rung.

LESSON 35

A. END OF THE VACATION

Как бы́стро лети́т вре́мя!	How quickly time flies.
Вот уже́ четы́ре неде́ли с тех пор, как я нача́ла путеше́ствовать.	[Here] it's four weeks already since I started to travel.
К сожале́нию, мой о́тпуск подхо́дит к концу́.	Unfortunately my vacation is coming to an end.
Мне ну́жно собира́ться.	I have to start packing.
У меня́ три чемода́на.	I have three suitcases.
Оди́н о́чень большо́й	One is very big, and

и два други́х поме́ньше.	the other two some-what smaller.
В большо́й чемода́н помеща́ется о́чень мно́го веще́й.	A great many things can be put into the big suitcase.
Но зато́ его́ о́чень тяжело́ нести́.	But on the other hand, it's very heavy to carry.
К сча́стью, мой друг пое́дет со мно́й на вокза́л.	Luckily, my friend will go to the station with me.
Он о́чень си́льный.	He's very strong.
Ему́ всё легко́.	Everything is light for him.
Ну́жно бу́дет купи́ть биле́ты зара́нее. Что́бы не стоя́ть в о́череди.	I'll have to buy tick-ets beforehand. In order not to stand on line [in turn].
Ну́жно не забы́ть позвони́ть всем знако́мым.	I [one] must not for-get to telephone all my friends.
Ну́жно бу́дет попроща́ться со все́ми.	I'll have to say good-bye to [take leave of] all of them.
Я сде́лала о́чень мно́го сни́мков и отдала́ их прояви́ть.	I took many pictures and left [gave] them to be developed.
Наде́юсь, что все фотогра́фии бу́дут гото́вы до моего́ отъе́зда.	I hope that all the pictures will be ready before my departure.
Я ещё не получи́ла бельё из сти́рки. Оно́ должно́ быть уже́ гото́во.	They still haven't brought my laundry. It should be ready by now.
Ну, вот ве́щи уже́	Well, my things are

уло́жены.	all packed.
За́втра мы е́дем домо́й. Коне́ц о́тпуску. До сле́дующего года.	Tomorrow we are going home. End to a vacation. Until next year.
В бу́дущем году́ мы опя́ть собира́емся пое́хать куда́-нибу́дь.	We are planning to go somewhere again next year.
Мне о́чень хо́чется пое́хать в Сре́днюю Азию.	I'd very much like to go to the Trans-caspian region.
Говоря́т, что там о́чень интере́сно.	They say [it is said] that it's very inter-esting there.
Там мно́го стари́нных городо́в.	There are many old cities there.
Наприме́р, го́род Ташке́нт де́лится на ста́рый го́род и но́вый го́род. Э́тот го́род изве́стен уже́ с седьмо́го ве́ка.	For instance, the city Tashkent is divided into the Old City and the New City. This city dates back to [is known from] the seventh century.
Там есть па́мятники дре́вней архитекту́ры пятна́дцатого и шестна́дцатого веко́в.	There are relics of ancient architecture of the fifteenth and sixteenth centuries.

QUIZ 24

1. Я просто не могу дождаться той минуты, когда передо мной будет море.

a. They say that this is very interesting.

2. В этом городе есть прекрасный вокзал и очень хороший ресторан.

b. From there, there is [opens up] an amazing view of the whole city.

3. Какое интересное
   совпадение!
4. Когда я вошел в ресторан,
   я встретил мою знакомую.
5. Вот свободный столик.

6. Говорят, что это очень
   интересно.
7. Давайте сядем здесь.

8. Оттуда открывается
   изумительный вид на
   весь город.
9. Поезд стоит здесь целый
   час.
10. Мне даже не верится,
    что я всё это увижу.
11. Пожалуйста, позвоните
    моей сестре и скажите,
    что вы встретили меня.
12. Я чуть не опоздал на
    свой поезд.
13. Как быстро летит время!

14. Я хочу купить газету.
15. К счастью, мой друг
    поедет со мной на
    вокзал.
16. Нужно не забыть
    позвонить всем знакомым.
17. Сколько стоит отправить
    письмо?

18. В будущем году мы опять
    поедем куда-нибудь.
19. Говорят, что там очень
    интересно.
20. Этот город известен
    уже с седьмого века.

c. I was almost late for my
   train.
d. The train stops here for a
   whole hour.
e. I'd like to buy a newspaper.
f. I must not forget to tele-
   phone all my friends.
g. Please call my sister and
   her that you met me.
h. How quickly time flies!

i. Luckily, my friend will
   go to the station with me.
j. How much is it for a
   letter?
k. They say that it's very
   interesting there.

l. Next year, again, we will
   go somewhere.
m. This city dates back to [is
   known from] the seventh
   century.
n. Let's sit here.
o. What an interesting
   coincidence!

p. Here's an empty table.
q. I simply can't wait for the
   moment when I'll see the
   ocean before [in front of]
   me.
r. I can hardly believe that
   will see all this.
s. In this city there is an
   excellent station and a
t. When I walked into the
   very good restaurant.
   restaurant, I met my
   friend.

LESSON 36

A. MAY OR CAN

The words "may" and "may not", and "can" and "cannot" are expressed in Russian by мо́жно (it is possible) and нельзя́ (it is not possible).

Мо́жно вы́йти?	May I go out?
Нет, нельзя́.	No, you may not.

Нельзя́ is a Russian word for which there is no English equivalent.

Мо́жно?	**Нельзя́**
May I?	No, you may not.
Can I?	No, you cannot.
Is it possible?	It is not impossible.
Is it allowed?	It is not allowed.

Нельзя́ сказа́ть, что здесь жа́рко.	You would not say that it is hot here.
Здесь нельзя́ кури́ть.	You [one] cannot (may not) smoke here.

Мо́жно and нельзя́ are adverbs and therefore do not change their form.

B. May I?

Саша:
Здесь мо́жно кури́ть?

Sasha:
May one smoke here?

Миша:
**Нет, здесь нельзя́
кури́ть. Посмотри́те,
вот там напи́сано:
«Кури́ть воспреща́ется».**

Misha:
No, (there's) no
smoking here. Look,
the sign says [it's
written there]:
"Smoking forbidden."

Саша:
**А где вообще́ мо́жно
кури́ть?**

Sasha:
Where can one
smoke?

Миша:
**В теа́трах мо́жно
кури́ть в фойе́. В
поезда́х есть
специа́льные ваго́ны
для куря́щих.**

Misha:
In theatres one may
smoke in the lobby.
In trains there are
special cars for
smokers.

Саша:
**У меня́ нет спи́чек.
Да́йте мне, пожа́луйста,
спи́чки. Ру́сские
сигаре́ты совсе́м не
таки́е, как
америка́нские.
К ним на́до
привы́кнуть.**

Sasha:
I have no matches.
Please give me
matches. Russian
cigarettes are not at
all like American
(cigarettes).
One must get used to
them.

Миша:
**Куре́ние вообще́ о́чень
плоха́я привы́чка.**

Misha:
Smoking is, in gener-
al, a very bad habit.

Саша:
**Соверше́нно с ва́ми
согла́сен, но я о́чень
люблю́ кури́ть.**

Sasha:
I completely agree
with you, but I love
to smoke.

Миша:
Вы уже́ вы́курили всю
  па́чку. Хва́тит на
  сего́дня.

Misha:
You've already fin-
  ished a whole pack.
  Enough for today.

Саша:
Ничего́ подо́бного. Я
  вы́курил то́лько
  полпа́чки.

Sasha:
Nothing of the sort.
  I smoked only half a
  pack.

Миша:
Пе́йте бо́льше молока́.
  Это вам о́чень поле́зно.

Misha:
Drink more milk. It's
  very good for you.

Саша:
Я не люблю́ пить и
  есть то, что поле́зно.

Sasha:
I don't like to drink
  and eat the things
  that are good for me.

Миша:
Вы что хоти́те, то и
  де́лаете!

Misha:
You do whatever
  you want!

Саша:
Коне́чно! Что хочу́, то
  и де́лаю.

Sasha:
Of course! What I
  want (to do), I do.

Миша:
Кури́ть мно́го—вре́дно,
  а пить мно́го молока́
  поле́зно.

Misha:
Smoking a lot is
  harmful, but drink-
  ing a lot of milk is
  good for you.

Саша:
Мо́жет бы́ть э́то и так,
  но я не люблю́ молока́.

Sasha:
Maybe that's so, but
  I don't like milk.

Миша:
Все де́ти выраста́ют на
  молоке́.

Misha:
All children grow up
  on milk.

Саша:
Когда́ я был ребёнком,
  я пил молоко́, а тепе́рь
  я курю́.

Sasha:
When I was a baby I
  drank milk, and now
  I smoke.

Миша:

**Вы свобо́дный челове́к.
Де́лайте, что хоти́те.**

Misha:

You're a free person.
Do as you please.

C. I CAN'T

**Мне нельзя́ выходи́ть.
Я простуди́лся. У меня́
боли́т го́рло и голова́.**

I can't go out. I
caught a cold. I have
a sore throat and a
headache.

**У вас на́сморк. Вам
ну́жно лежа́ть в
посте́ли. До́ктор
сказа́л, что вам
нельзя́ кури́ть.**

You have a head
cold. You have to
stay in bed. The doc-
tor said that you
can't smoke.

**На э́тот конце́рт
нельзя́ попа́сть; все
биле́ты про́даны.**

It's impossible to get
to that concert. All
the tickets have been
sold.

**О́чень жа́ль, что
нельзя́. Пойдём
куда́-нибудь в друго́е
ме́сто.**

Too bad that it's
impossible. Let's go
somewhere else.

**Ему́ нельзя́ ходи́ть
по ле́стнице. У него́
сла́бое се́рдце.**

He can't walk up
stairs. He has a weak
heart.

**Он живёт как нельзя́
лу́чше.**

One can't live any
better than he does.

**Где ваш друг Никола́й
сего́дня?**

Where is your friend
Nicholas today?

**Я никогда́ не зна́ю,
где он.**

I never know where
he is [could be].

QUIZ 25

1. Вы что хотите, то и
   делаете.
2. Курить много вредно,

a. They have everything
   you need.
b. What does this word

а пить много молока полезно.

3. Нельзя сказать, что это всегда так.

4. На этот концерт нельзя попасть, все билеты проданы.

5. Ему нельзя ходить по лестнице. У него слабое сердце.

6. Он живёт, как нельзя лучше.

7. От кого вы получили письмо?

8. С кем вы были в театре вчера?

9. Что значит это слово?

10. Чего только нет в этом магазине!

11. Не понимаю–о чём тут говорить?

12. Как вы себя чувствуете?

13. У них есть всё, что вам нужно.

14. Мне хочется пить.

15. Я могу сказать только несколько слов по-русски.

16. Вы плохо произносите русские слова.

17. Мне трудно понимать, когда вы говорите так быстро.

18. Простите, но я не понимаю вас.

19. Какое вино вы хотите белое или красное?

20. Куда вы идёте обедать– после работы?

mean?

c. I can say only a few words in Russian.

d. What they don't have in this store!

e. You pronounce Russian words badly.

f. I don't understand–what is there to talk about?

g. I'm thirsty.

h. What kind of wine do you want–white or red?

i. Excuse me, but I don't understand you.

j. Where are you going to have dinner after work?

k. You do everything that you want to do.

l. It's difficult for me to understand when you speak so fast.

m. One can't live any better than he does

n. With whom were you in the theatre yesterday?

o. Smoking a lot is harmful, but drinking a lot of milk is good for you.

p. From whom did you get a letter?

q. It's impossible to get to that concert. All the tickets have been sold.

r. He can't walk up stairs. He has a weak heart.

s. How are you feeling?

t. You [one] can't say that it is always so.

ANSWERS
1–k; 2–o; 3–t; 4–q; 5–r; 6–m; 7–p; 8–n; 9–b; 10–d; 11–f; 12–s;
13–a; 14–g; 15–c; 16–e; 17–l 18–i; 19–h; 20–j.

LESSON 37

A. LOST AND FOUND

Мы не зна́ли доро́ги и потеря́ли мно́го вре́мени по доро́ге в музе́й.	We didn't know the way and lost a lot of time on the way to the museum.
Он потеря́л свой бума́жник.	He lost his wallet.
Об э́том ну́жно заяви́ть милиционе́ру или пря́мо в мили́цию.	You must report that to a policeman or go directly to the police station.
Если кто́-нибудь найдёт э́тот бума́жник, то его́, по всей вероя́тности, верну́т.	If someone finds this wallet, he will, in all probability, return it.
Она́ ничего́ никогда́ не теря́ет.	She never loses anything.
Вчера́ она́ потеря́ла одну́ перча́тку.	Yesterday she lost one glove.
Кто́-то её нашёл.	Someone found it.
Она́ лежи́т тепе́рь на столе́ у администра́тора гости́ницы.	It's now lying on the hotel manager's desk.
Когда́ я хожу́ пешко́м по у́лице, я всегда́ что́-нибудь нахожу́.	When I walk along the street, I always find something.
Сего́дня я нашёл о́чень хоро́шую авторучку.	Today I found a very good fountain pen.

Мне так жаль того, кто её потеря́л.	I'm so sorry for the one who lost it.
Что вы и́щете?	What are you looking for?
Я всегда́ что́-нибудь ищу́.	I am always looking for something.
Ищи́те—и вы найдёте.	Seek, and you will find.
В Москве́ не тру́дно найти́ хоро́ший теа́тр.	In Moscow it's not difficult to find a good theatre.
Я потеря́лся и не знал, куда́ идти́.	I lost my way and didn't know where to go.
Я потеря́лся и не знал что сказа́ть.	I became flustered and didn't know what to say.
Я заблуди́лся и не мог найти́ доро́ги.	I got lost and couldn't find the road.
В э́том го́роде о́чень не тру́дно заблуди́ть-ся.	It's not difficult to lose one's way in this city.
Э́то о́чень ста́рый го́род. У́лицы у́зкие и кривы́е, и никогда́ не изве́стно куда́ у́лица повернёт и куда́ она́ вас приведёт.	This is a very old city. The streets are narrow and crooked, and you never know where the street turns and where it will lead you.
Ма́ленькие у́зкие у́лицы называ́ются по-ру́сски переу́лками.	Little narrow streets are called "pereulok" in Russian.
В го́роде, где я когда́-то жил, была́ у́лица, кото́рая	In the city where I lived one time, there was a street

называлась
«Театральный переу-
лок».

that was called
"Theatre Pereulok"
[Theatre Lane].

Если переулок не
проходной то он
называется тупиком.

If a pereulok has a
dead end, it is called
a "tupik."

Очень часто говорят:
Я попал в тупик. Это
значит, что вы в
таком положении, из
которого нет выхода.
Надеюсь, что никто
из нас никогда не
попадёт в тупик.

Very often it is said:
"I got into a tupik."
This means that you
are in the kind of
situation that has no
way out. I hope that
not one of us ever
falls into a tupik.

Из каждого тупика
можно выйти тем же
путём, каким вы в
него вошли.

It is possible to get out
of every tupik by the
same road through
which you entered.

Иногда нужно
сделать шаг назад.
Все мы делаем иногда
ошибки.

Sometimes it is neces-
sary to take a step
backward. We all
make mistakes some-
times.

Не ошибается только
тот, кто ничего не
делает.

Only he who does
nothing makes no
mistakes.

Я ошибся и пошёл
направо, а надо было
идти налево.

I made a mistake and
turned to the right,
and I should have
gone to the left.

Очень трудно
говорить без ошибок.

It's very difficult to
speak without mis-
takes.

Очень трудно писать
без ошибок.

It's very difficult to
write without mis-
takes.

Легко́ де́лать то́лько то, что вы хорошо́ зна́ете.	It's only easy to do that which you know well.
Рабо́тайте, занима́йтесь, слу́шайте, повторя́йте, чита́йте, запомина́йте.	Work, study, listen, repeat, read, memorize.
Вы́учите всё, что на э́тих плёнках и вы бу́дете говори́ть по-ру́сски.	Learn everything that is on these tapes, and you will speak Russian.

B. THE IMPERATIVE MOOD

The imperative of a verb is formed from the second-person singular present tense. For the singular imperative, replace the ending with й if the ending is a vowel, with и if the ending is a consonant (and the first-person singular form of the verb is stressed on the ending), and with ь if the ending is a consonant (but the first-person singular form is not stressed on the ending). For the plural imperative, add те to the singular.

INFINITIVE	SECOND-PERS. SINGULAR	FAMILAR, SINGULAR	PLURAL, POLITE
писа́ть to write	пи́ш-ешь	пиши́!	пиши́те!
повторя́ть to repeat	повторя́-ешь	повторя́й!	повторя́йте!
броса́ть to throw	броса́-ешь	брось!	бро́сьте!
рабо́тать to work	рабо́та-ешь	рабо́тай!	рабо́тайте!
чита́ть to read	чита́-ешь	чита́й!	чита́йте!

The reflexive verb retains its endings:–ся after a consonant or after -й, and -сь after vowel.

мы́ться	мо́-ешься	мо́йся!	мо́йтесь!
to wash			
(oneself)			
занима́ться	занима́-ешься	занима́йся!	занима́йтесь!
to study			

In giving an order indirectly to a third person, the forms пусть and пуска́й are used with the third-person singular of the verb:

| Пусть он чита́ет. | Let him read. | [He should read.] |
| Пуска́й она́ говори́т. | Let her speak. | [She should speak.] |

C. Even More On Perfective and Imperfective Verbs

This lesson again shows the use of perfective and imperfective verbs:

Imperfective	Perfective
теря́ть	потеря́ть
находи́ть	найти

Он потеря́л свой бума́жник.	He lost his wallet (once, this time: perfective).
Она́ ничего́ никогда́ не теря́ет.	She never loses anything (at any time: imperfective).
Я всегда́ что́-нибудь нахожу́.	I always find things (all the time: imperfective).
Сего́дня я нашёл...	Today I found (one time, one action: perfective)...

D. WORD STUDY

голова́	head
ва́жный	important
вопро́с	question, issue
по́здно	late
де́ло	matter, business
коне́чно	of course
за́втра	tomorrow
ско́ро	soon
да́льше	further

QUIZ 26

1. Я никуда не иду после обеда.

2. Чья газета там на столе?

3. Когда я хожу пешком по улице, я всегда что-нибудь нахожу.

4. Как называется этот город?

5. Я потерялся и не знал что сказать.

6. Как вам не стыдно так скоро забыть меня!

7. Сегодня я нашёл очень хорошую авторучку.

8. Как я рад, что встретил вас!

9. Это как раз то, что мне надо.

10. Это гораздо труднее, чем вы думаете.

11. Возможно, что вы правы.

12. Мне так жаль того, кто её потерял

a. You may be right.

b. All the best, and have a pleasant trip.

c. It's not difficult to lose one's way in this city.

d. It is possible to get out of every blind alley by the same road through which you entered in.

e. Tupik is a situation that has no way out.

f. When I came here, I had two hundred rubles.

g. I am so sorry for the one who lost it.

h. I lost my way and didn't know where to go.

i. Aren't you ashamed to have forgotten me so soon!

j. I became flustered and didn't know what to say.

k. Whose newspaper is that on the table?

l. How glad I am that I met you!

13. Мне нужно идти. Мой поезд сейчас отходит.	m. I am not going anywhere after dinner.
14. Всего хорошего и счастливого пути.	n. Today I found a very good fountain pen.
15. Я потерялся и не знал куда идти.	o. It's just the thing I need.
16. В этом городе очень нетрудно заблудиться.	p. Only he who does nothing makes no mistakes.
17. Из каждого тупика можно выйти тем же путем, каким вы в него вошли.	q. What is the name of this city?
18. Тупик–это положение, из которого нет выхода.	r. It's far more difficult than you think.
19. Когда я приехал сюда, у меня было двести рублей.	s. I have to go. My train is leaving immediately.
20. Не ошибается только тот, кто ничего не делает.	t. When I walk along the street, I always find something.

ANSWERS

1–m; 2–k; 3–t; 4–q; 5–j; 6–i; 7–n; 8–l; 9–o; 10–r; 11–a; 12–g; 13–s; 14–b; 15–h; 16–c; 17–d; 18–e; 19–f; 20–p.

LESSON 38

A. BUYING GIFTS

Ольга:

Я сегодня иду в магазин. Мне нужно кое-что купить. Хотите пойти со мной?

Игорь:

Мне что-то не хочется, но я думаю, что я всё же пойду.

Olga:

I'm going to the store today. I have to buy something. Do you want to go with me?

Igor:

I don't feel like it, but I think I'll go anyway. What store do you want

В какой магазин вы хотите пойти?

to go to?

Ольга:

Olga:

Я хочу пойти в магазин, который называется «Детский мир». Там есть всё для детей любого возраста.

I want to go to a store called "Children's World." There they have everything for children of any age.

Игорь:

Igor:

Ну, если так, то я пойду с вами.

Oh, if that's so, then I'll go with you.

Ольга:

Olga:

Вот и хорошо. Мне нужно купить юбку племяннице и какую-нибудь игрушку сыну.

That's fine. I have to buy a skirt for my niece and some toy for my son.

Игорь:

Igor:

Какой большой магазин! Как здесь интересно.

What a big store! How interesting it is here.

Ольга:

Olga:

Пойдёмте на второй этаж. Там продают юбки.

Let's go to the second floor. That's where skirts are sold.

Игорь:

Igor:

Вот очень красивая юбка. Вам нравится?

There's a very pretty skirt. Do you like it?

Ольга:

Olga:

Нет не очень. Мне не нравится этот цвет. Слишком яркий.

Not very much. I don't like that color. It's too bright.

Игорь:

Igor:

Да что вы! Совсем нет! Ведь ваша

Oh, what do you mean! No, it's not! [not at all!]

племя́нница така́я
молода́я де́вушка.

Why, your niece is still
so young!

Ольга:

Olga:

Да, коне́чно. Но она́
о́чень скро́мная и
предпочита́ет
что́-нибудь попро́ще.
Вот э́та се́рая ю́бка
бу́дет лу́чше, пра́вда?

Yes, of course. But she is
very modest and prefers
something simpler.
Here, this gray skirt will
be better, don't you
think?

Игорь:

Igor:

Соверше́нно ве́рно.

Quite right.

Ольга:

Olga:

Де́вушка, ско́лько
сто́ит э́та ю́бка?

Young lady, how much
does this skirt cost?

Продавец:

Salesperson:

Два́дцать рубле́й. Э́то
чи́стая ше́рсть. И
о́чень хорошо́
но́сится.

Twenty rubles. It's pure
wool. And wears very
well.

Ольга:

Olga:

Да? Я её возьму́. Я
покупа́ю не для
себя́ и е́сли разме́р
не подойдёт, мо́жно
бу́дет поменя́ть?

Yes? I'll take it. I'm not
buying it for myself, so
if the size isn't right,
may I exchange it?

Продавец:

Salesperson:

Коне́чно, в любо́е
вре́мя. То́лько не в
воскресе́нье. По
воскресе́ньям наш
магази́н закры́т. Э́то
наш выходно́й день.

Of course. At any time.
But not on Sunday. Our
store is closed on
Sundays. That's our day
off.

Игорь:

Igor:

А почему́ у них
выходно́й день в
воскресе́нье?

But why do they have
their day off on
Sunday?

Ольга:	*Olga:*
В Росси́и в воскресе́нье все магази́ны закры́ты.	In Russia all stores are closed on Sunday.
Игорь:	*Igor:*
Вы ещё ничего́ не купи́ли ва́шему сы́ну.	You haven't bought anything for your son yet.
Ольга:	*Olga:*
Ах да! Вот о́чень хоро́шие ку́бики. Он о́чень лю́бит стро́ить. Ско́лько сто́ят э́ти ку́бики?	Oh, yes. Here are some very nice blocks. He loves to build. How much are these blocks?
Продавец:	*Salesperson:*
Три́дцать рубле́й.	Thirty rubles.
Ольга:	*Olga:*
Это до́рого, но я всё же их возьму́. Вот три́дцать рубле́й.	That's a little expensive, but I'll take them anyway. Here are thirty rubles.
Продавец:	*Salesperson:*
Не забу́дьте, пожа́луйста, ва́шу сда́чу.	Don't forget your change, please.
Игорь/Ольга:	*Igor/Olga:*
До свида́ния. Спаси́бо.	Good-bye. Thank you.

B. Use of the Particles To and Нибудь

кто́-то	someone	кто́-нибудь	anyone
где́-то	somewhere	где́-нибудь	anywhere
что́-то	something	что́-нибудь	anything
куда́-то	somewhere	куда́-нибудь	anywhere
почему́-то	for some reason	почему́-нибудь	for any reason

To is used to show that something is known:

Кто́-то пришёл.
  Someone came. (I don't know who, but someone did come.)

Он куда́-то пое́дет за́втра.
  He is going someplace tomorrow. (I don't know where, but he does, and it is definite that he is going.)

Нибудь is used to show that nothing is known:

Кто́-нибудь придёт.
  Somebody will come. (I don't know who it will be, I don't know if anyone will come, but I think that somebody will come.)

Мне хо́чется куда́-нибудь пое́хать.
  I feel like going someplace. (I don't know where and I don't know if I will, but I feel like it.)

QUIZ 27

1. Я встаю в восемь часов утра.
2. Этот костюм стоит семьдесят пять рублей.
3. Вы ещё ничего не купили вашему сыну.
4. Покажите мне, пожалуйста, эту книгу.
5. Мне не нравится этот цвет. Слишком яркий.
6. Вот эта серая юбка будет лучше, правда?
7. По воскресеньям наш магазин закрыт.

a. On Sundays our store is closed.
b. It's a question of taste.
c. He doesn't want to do anything.
d. He prefers something simpler.
e. The performance starts at a quarter of eight.
f. How often do the buses run?
g. What delicious pastry!

8. Это дорого, но я всё же их возьму.

9. Не забудьте, пожалуйста, вашу сдачу.

10. Мне очень нравится этот город.

11. Я всегда пью кофе с молоком.

12. Это дело вкуса.

13. Какое вкусное пирожное!

14. Спектакль начинается без четверти восемь.

15. Он ничего не хочет делать.

16. Она была в магазине и ничего не купила.

17. Он предпочитает что-нибудь попроще.

18. Как часто ходят троллейбусы?

19. Каждые пять минут.

20. Вы не знаете, что сегодня идёт в театре?

h. I get up at eight o'clock in the morning.

i. She was in the store and didn't buy anything.

j. Every five minutes.

k. This suit costs seventy-five rubles.

l. You haven't bought anything for your son yet.

m. Do you know what is playing at the theatre today?

n. I don't like that color. It's too bright.

o. It's expensive, but I'll take them anyway.

p. I like this city very much.

q. Here, this gray skirt will be better, don't you think [isn't it true]?

r. I always drink coffee with milk.

s. Don't forget your change, please.

t. Please, show me this book.

ANSWERS

1–h; 2–k; 3–l; 4–t; 5–n; 6–q; 7–a; 8–o; 9–s; 10–p; 11–r; 12–b; 13–g; 14–e; 15–c; 16–i; 17–d; 18–f; 19–j; 20–m.

LESSON 39

A. Two colleagues

Илья:
Здравствуйте, милая
  Надежда Георгиевна!

Ilya:
Hello, dear Nadezhda
  Georgievna!

Надежда:
Здравствуйте, Илья
  Петрович! Как я
  рада вас видеть! Я
  как раз собиралась
  вам позвонить.

Nadezhda:
How are you, Ilya
  Petrovich! I am so
  happy to see you. I was
  just about to call you.

Илья:
А что такое?

Ilya:
What's the matter?

Надежда:
У меня в субботу
  будет приём.
  Приезжает группа
  коммерсантов
  из России. С
  некоторыми из них
  вы уже знакомы по
  работе в банке.
  Помните Василия
  Смирнова и Николая
  Радзинского?

Nadezhda:
I am having a reception
  on Saturday. A group
  of businessmen from
  Russia is coming. Some
  of them you already
  know through your
  work at the bank.
  Do you remember
  Vasily Smirnov and
  Nikolai Radzinsky?

Илья:
Да, да, конечно. Как
  я могу вам помочь?

Ilya:
Yes, yes, of course. How
  can I help you?

Надежда:
Даже неловко просить.
  Дело в том, что
  Джим, мой муж,
  заинтересован в
  организации

Nadezhda:
It's awkward to even ask.
  The thing is that Jim,
  my husband, is
  interested in organizing
  a joint venture in

совмéстного предприя́тия в Одéссе. Но нужна́ подде́ржка мéстных власте́й. Тепéрь, конéчно, э́то ужé Украи́на, и всё осложня́ется. Крóме тогó, Джим óчень плóхо говори́т по-рýсски. Корóче, нужны́ перевóдчики. Я, конéчно, сама́ бýду переводи́ть, но грýппа больша́я. В óбщем, сáми понима́ете.

Odessa. But the support of local authorities is what is needed. Now, of course, it's already Ukraine, and everything is becoming complicated. Besides, Jim's Russian is very bad. In short, we need interpreters. I will certainly interpret myself, but the group is large. Well, you understand.

Илья́:

Надéжда Геóргиевна! О чём речь! Вы же знáете, что я всегда́ готóв помóчь. Да, к томý же, я сам переговори́ть с Радзи́нским насчёт капиталовложéний в рýсские кооперати́вы.

Ilya:

Nadezhda Georgievna! What are you talking about! You know that I am always ready to help. Besides, I wanted to have a chat with Radzinsky myself about investments in Russian cooperatives.

Надéжда:

Ну и слáва Бóгу! В óбщем, ждý вас у себя́ в 7 часóв. Я заказáла пирожки́, икрý и, конéчно, я́щик шампáнского и рýсскую вóдку.

Nadezhda:

Thank God. So I am expecting you at my place at seven o'clock. I ordered meat pies, caviar, a case of champagne and Russian vodka.

Илья:
Пока перевожу,
  придётся без водки
  обойтись.

Ilya:
I will have to do without
  vodka while interpreting.

Надежда:
Конечно, конечно.
  Огромное спасибо.
  Жду.

Nadezhda:
Of course, of course.
  I am very grateful. I'm
  expecting you.

B. AT THE MUSEUM

I. Nina asks the way to the Hermitage:

Нина: Извините, пожалуйста. Как дойти до
Эрмитажа?
Nina: Excuse me, how can I get to the Hermitage?

Прохожий: Да это недалеко отсюда. Идите
прямо, и музей будет слева от вас.
Passer-by: It's not far from here. Go straight ahead,
and the museum will be on the left.

Нина: Спасибо. Можно дойти пешком?
Nina: Thanks. So I can walk there?

Прохожий: Да, конечно! Желаю вам приятно
провести время в Петербурге.
Passer-by: Yes, of course! Have a pleasant stay in
St. Petersburg.

II. Nina goes to the Hermitage with her friend Ivan:

Нина: Знаете, я очень интересуюсь русским
искусством.
Nina: You know, I'm very interested in Russian art.

Иван: Я то́же! Я интересу́юсь анти́чным и средневеко́вым иску́сством.
Ivan: Me too! I'm interested in antiques and medieval art.

Како́й ваш люби́мый пери́од?
What period do you like the best?

Ни́на: Я обожа́ю передви́жников! Смотри́те! Вот карти́на худо́жника-передви́жника. Кто её написа́л?
Nina: I love the Wanderers (*the Peredvizhniki*)! Look! There's a picture by one of the Wandering painters! Who painted it?

Ива́н: Это карти́на Ре́пина.
Ivan: That's by Repin.

Ни́на: Да, ве́рно. В како́м году́ он её написа́л?
Nina: Oh, yes. What year did he complete it?

Ива́н: Одну́ мину́точку. Я посмотрю́...В ты́сяча восемьсо́т во́семьдесят четвёртом году́.
Ivan: Just a moment. I'll look... in 1884.

LESSON 40

A. PROBLEMS OF THE PLANET

Проблемы планеты.

Необдуманные индустриальные проекты часто ведут к нарушению экологического баланса на земле. Поэтому за последние несколько лет всё больше людей в мире начинают выступать за охрану природы.

Большую тревогу вызывает потепление климата. 1988 год был самым тёплым на планете за последние сто лет, а шесть из десяти самых тёплых лет в этом столетии приходятся на восьмидесятые годы. В начале нынешнего века средняя температура была гораздо ниже, чем теперь.

Ученые пока не могут назвать точной причины потепления земного климата. Может быть это связано с разрушением озонового слоя атмосферы. Это происходит, когда фреоны и другие синтетические вещества, содержащие хлор, поступают в атмосферу.

Русские специалисты нашли замену фреону: это соединение пропана и бутана, безвредное для атмосферного слоя. Кроме того, планируется полное прекращение выпуска фреонов российской химической промышленностью. Россия принимает серьёзные меры для разрешения проблемы разрушения озонового слоя.

Обычные люди тоже могут помочь в этом

деле. Для этого нужно прекратить
пользоваться косметикой, в которой
распылителем служат фреоны, реже включать
кондиционер, и покупать качественные
холодильники. Мы все должны участвовать в
охране природы.

Thoughtless industrial projects often lead to dis-
turbance of the ecological balance on earth.
Therefore, in recent years, more and more people in
the world have begun to speak out in support of
protecting nature.

Warming of the climate (global warming) causes
great alarm. 1988 was the warmest year on the planet in one hundred years[1], and six out of the ten
warmest years in this century have occurred in the
eighties. Early in this century the average tempera-
ture was much lower than it is now.

Scientists cannot yet name the exact reason for
the warming of the earth's climate. Perhaps it is
related to the destruction of the ozone layer in the
atmosphere. This happens when Freons and other
synthetic compounds containing chlorine enter the
atmosphere.

Russian specialists found a substitute for
Freons:–a compound of propane and butane, which
is harmless to the atmospheric layer. Moreover, a
complete halt in the production of Freons by the
Russian chemical industry is being planned. Russia
is taking serious measures to solve the problem of
the destruction of the ozone layer.

Ordinary people can also help in this matter. For
example, it is necessary to stop using cosmetic
products in which Freons are propellants, to turn air-

[1] as of this writing

conditioning on less often, and to buy refrigerators of good quality. We should all participate in the protection of nature.

B. PARTICIPLES AND GERUNDS

Participles and gerunds are very important parts of the Russian language, so it is necessary to know how to recognize and to understand them. However, it should be made clear that they are not used very much in simple conversation, but rather in literature and scientific writing.

Participles are verbal adjectives; gerunds are verbal adverbs. Participles are adjectives made out of verbs. The difference between an adjective and a participle is in tense; i.e., participles can be present or past tense, active or passive voice. They retain this verbal quality. In every other respect they are adjectives. They have three genders: masculine, feminine, neuter. They decline like adjectives and agree with the words they modify in gender, case, and number.

	PRESENT PARTICIPLE	PAST PARTICIPLE
говори́ть	говоря́щий, ая, ее, ие	говори́вший, ая, ее, ие

PREPOSITIONAL PLURAL:

Мы говори́м о говоря́щих по-англи́йски ученика́х.

We are talking about students who speak English.

Gerunds are verbal adverbs and as such do not change, but have present and past tenses. The present tense is formed from the imperfective; the past tense must be formed from the perfective. The present tense is characterized by two actions at the same time. In the past tense there are two actions, one following the other; when the first action is completed, the second one starts.

PRESENT TENSE:
читáть

Читáя, он улыбáлся.
While reading, he was smiling. (The two actions are simultaneous.)

PAST TENSE:
прочитáть

Прочитáв газéту, он встал и ушёл.
Having finished reading the paper, he got up and went away. (One action follows the other.)

FINAL REVIEW

1. Я хочу хорошо _____ по-русски. I want to speak Russian well.
2. Кто _____ это? Who said that?
3. _____ вы хотите видеть? Whom do you wish to see?
4. _____ вы дали мою книгу? Whom did you give my book to?
5. С _____ вы были в театре вчера? Whom were you with in the theatre yesterday?
6. Это всё, _____ он сказал. That's all that he said.
7. Для _____ это? What's this for?
8. На _____ вы сидите? What are you sitting on?
9. У _____ нет карандаша. I don't have a pencil.
10. О _____ вы говорили? Whom were you talking about?
11. Есть у _____ карта Москвы? Have you a map of Moscow?
12. Вот _____ магазин. Here's a good store.
13. Я _____ пить. I want a [to] drink.
14. У _____ есть всё. They have everything.
15. _____ удивляетесь? What are you surprised at?
16. У _____ нет брата. She has no brother.
17. Мне _____ пить. I'm thirsty. [I feel like drinking.]

18. Я _____ по-русски. I speak Russian.
19. Мы _____ читать. We want to read.
20. Они _____ хорошо. They understand well.
21. Вы говорите слишком _____ . You speak too fast.
22. Пожалуйста, говорите _____ . Please speak slower.
23. _____ я понимаю. Now I understand.
24. _____ времени? What time is it?
25. Он _____ домой. He goes home (on foot).
26. Мы _____ обедать дома. We will have dinner at home.
27. Как вас _____ . What is your name?
28. Как _____ этот город? What is the name of this city?
29. Спасибо, я _____ не хочу. Thank you, I don't want any more.
30. _____ сегодня число? What is today's date?
31. Мне очень _____ эта книга. I like this book very much.
32. Он _____ весь вечер. He spoke all evening.
33. Он _____ всё, что он знал. He said all he knew (perfective).
34. У меня дома много _____ . I have a lot of books at home.
35. Я хочу _____ молока. I want some more milk.
36. Завтра я _____ письмо брату. Tomorrow I will write a letter to my brother.
37. _____ она красивая! How pretty she is!
38. Он встаёт _____ каждый день. He gets up early every day.
39. Она _____ в Москве. She lived in Moscow.
40. Дети _____ по-русски. The children will speak Russian (imperfective).
41. Вчера мы читали _____ . We read the paper yesterday.
42. _____ ему, что я буду у него дома завтра. Tell him that I will be at his house tomorrow.
43. _____ войти? May I come in?
44. Он взял книгу и _____ . He took the book and went away.
45. Он всегда всё _____ . He always forgets everything.
46. Здесь _____ курить. No smoking here.
47. Он ничего _____ . He knows nothing. [He doesn't know anything.]
48. Он никогда _____ в Москве. He was never in Moscow.

49. Доктор сказал, что вам _____ курить. The doctor said that you can't smoke.
50. Всё _____ , что _____ кончается. All's well that ends well.
51. Я иду на _____ . I am going to the office.
52. Мой брат работает _____ . My brother works at home.
53. Мы живём в _____ . We live in town.
54. Он пишет _____ . He is writing with a pencil.
55. Я смотрю на _____ . I am looking at my brother.
56. Он любит читать _____ . He likes to read newspapers.
57. У меня нет _____ _____ . I don't have black pencils.
58. Мы говорим о моём _____ . We are talking about my friend.
59. У него нет _____ . He has no sister.
60. Он пишет письмо _____ . He is writing a letter to his wife.

ANSWERS

1. говорить	2. сказал	3. кого
4. кому	5. кем	6. что
7. чего	8. чём	9. меня
10. ком	11. вас	12. хороший
13. хочу	14. них	15. чему
16. неё	17. хочется	18. говорю
19. хотим	20. понимают	21. быстро
22. медленнее	23. теперь	24. сколько
25. идёт	26. будем	27. зовут
28. называется	29. больше	30. какое
31. нравится	32. говорил	33. сказал
34. книг	35. ещё	36. напишу
37. какая	38. рано	39. жила
40. будут говорить	41. газету	42. скажите
43. можно	44. ушёл	45. забывает
46. нельзя	47. не знает	48. не был
49. нельзя	50. хорошо хорошо	51. работу
52. дома	53. городе	54. карандашом

55. брата	56. газеты	57. чёрных каран- дашей
58. друге	59. сестры	60. жене

SUMMARY OF RUSSIAN GRAMMAR

1. THE RUSSIAN ALPHABET

Russian Letter	Script		Name
Аа	*A*	*a*	*ah*
Бб	*Б*	*б*	*beh*
Вв	*В*	*в*	*veh*
Гг	*Г*	*г*	*geh*
Дд	*D*	*g*	*deh*
Ее	*Е*	*е*	*yeh*
Ёё	*Ё*	*ё*	*yoh*
Жж	*Ж*	*ж*	*zheh*
Зз	*З*	*з*	*zeh*
Ии	*И*	*и*	*ee*
Йй	*Й*	*й*	*ee* (*i* short)
Кк	*К*	*к*	*kah*
Лл	*Л*	*л*	*ell*
Мм	*М*	*м*	*em*
Нн	*Н*	*н*	*en*
Оо	*О*	*о*	*oh*
Пп	*П*	*п*	*peh*
Рр	*Р*	*р*	*err*
Сс	*С*	*с*	*ess*
Тт	*Т*	*т*	*teh*
Уу	*У*	*у*	*ooh*
Фф	*Ф*	*ф*	*eff*

Xx	*X*	*x*	*khah*
Цц	*Ц*	*ц*	*tseh*
Чч	*Ч*	*ч*	*cheh*
Шш	*Ш*	*ш*	*shah*
Щщ	*Щ*	*щ*	*shchah*
Ыы	*Ы*	*ы*	*yerih*
Ьь	*Ь*	*ь*	*soft sign*
Ъъ	*Ъ*	*ъ*	*hard sign*
Ээ	*Э*	*э*	*eh*
Юю	*Ю*	*ю*	*yuh*
Яя	*Я*	*я*	*yah*

2. Pronunciation

VOWELS

The letter **a**, when stressed, is pronounced like the English *ah*; when unstressed before a stressed syllable, **a** is pronounced *ah*, but shorter, and in most other positions is given a neuter sound.

The letter **o**, when stressed, is pronounced like the English *oh*; when unstressed in first place before the stressed syllable or used initially, **o** is pronounced *ah*, and in all other positions has a neuter sound.

The letter **y** is pronounced both stressed and unstressed like the English *ooh*.

The letter **ы** is pronounced everywhere like the sound between the letters *b* and *l* in *table*.

The letter **э** is pronounced like the *eh* in *echo*.

Five vowels–**e**, **ё**, **и**, **ю**, **я**–have a glide (the sound similar to the final sound in the English word "may") in front of them. The function of these vowels is the palatalization of the preceding consonant, to which they lose the above-mentioned glide. However, when they follow a vowel or soft or hard signs, or when they appear in the initial position of a word, they are pronounced as in the alphabet–i.e. , with an initial glide.

The letter и always palatalizes the preceding consonant and is pronounced like the *ee* in *beet*, except when it follows the letters ж, ц, ш, which are never palatalized, when it is pronounced like the Russian sound ы.

The letter й is never stressed. It is pronounced like the final sound in *boy*.

The letter е always palatalizes the consonant that precedes it, except when that consonant is ж, ц, ш. When stressed, it is pronounced like the *eh* in *echo*, losing its glide to the palatalization of the preceding consonant; in unstressed positions it is pronounced like the *ee* in *beet*. Initially, it is pronounced with the glide: stressed, like *yeh*; unstressed, like *yeeh*.

The letter ё always palatalizes the preceding consonant, and is always stressed. It is pronounced *aw* and retains its glide when used initially, being pronounced *yaw*.

The letter я always palatalizes the preceding consonant; when stressed, it is pronounced *ah*; when unstressed, it is pronounced like the neuter sound of *a* in *sofa*. Initially, it retains its glide; when stressed, it is pronounced *yah,* when unstressed, *yee*.

The letter ю always palatalizes the preceding consonant. It is pronounced *ooh* in the body of the word; initially it retains its glide and is pronounced *yooh*.

The letter ь is called the "soft" sign; it palatalizes the preceding consonant, allowing the following vowel to retain its glide.

The letter ъ is called the "hard" sign. It indicates that the preceding consonant remains hard and that the following vowel retains its glide.

CONSONANTS

As in every language, Russian consonants may be voiced or voiceless. The pairs are:

English		Russian
б в г д ж з	(voiced)	b v g d j z
п ф к т ш с	(voiceless)	p f k t sh s

When two consonants are pronounced together, they must both be either voiced or voiceless. In Russian, the second one always remains as it is, and the first one changes accordingly:

всё, все, вчера́;   в=v; pronounced *f*

сде́лать, сдать;   с=s; pronounced *z*

The preposition в (in) is very often pronounced *f:*

в шко́ле is pronounced *fshkaw - lee.*

All consonants are voiceless at the end of a word. All consonants can also be hard or soft (i.e., palatalized or nonpalatalized) when followed by the letters, е, ё, и, ю, я or ь. Only the consonants ж, ц, and ш are always hard.

3. GENDER

All Russian nouns, pronouns, adjectives, and ordinal numbers, as well as some cardinal numbers and even several verb forms have gender: masculine, feminine, or neuter. In the plural there is only one form for all genders.

MASCULINE	FEMININE	NEUTER	PLURAL

Most nouns and pronouns and the past tense of verbs end on:

hard consonant а, я	о, е	а, ы, и

Most adjectives, ordinal numbers, and participles end on:

ой, ый, ий	ая, яя	ое, ее	ые, ие

NOTICE

Pronouns, adjectives, and ordinal numbers always agree in gender with the nouns they modify or represent.

4. CASES

a. With few exceptions, all nouns, pronouns, and adjectives decline. Each declension has six cases:

Nominative:	Кто? Что?	Who? What?
Genitive:	Кого? Чего?	Whom? What?
	От кого? От чего?	From whom From What?,,
	У кого? У чего?	At or by whom (what)?
	Без кого? Без чего?	Without whom (what)?
Dative:	Кому? Чему?	To whom? To what?
	К кому? К чему?	To whom? To what?
Accusative:	Кого? Что?	Whom? What?
	Куда?	Where (direction toward)?
Instrumental:	Кем? Чем?	By whom? By what?
	С кем? С чем?	With whom? With what?
Prepositional	О ком? О чём?	About whom? About what?

| or Locative: | В ком? В чём? | In whom? In what? |
| | Где? | Where (location)? |

b. Overall characteristics of the cases and most used prepositions:

1. The nominative case supplies the subject of the sentence.

2. The genitive case is the case of possession and negation. It is also used with many prepositions, the most common of which are:

без	without
для	for
до	up to
из	out of
около	about
от	from
после	after
у	at or by

3. The dative case is used in the meaning of to whom. Prepositions governing the dative case are:

| к | to |
| по | along |

4. The acccusative is the direct object case. Prepositions used with this case include:

в	to, into
за	behind
на	to, into, on (direction)

5. The instrumental case indicates the manner of action or instrument with which the action is performed. Prepositions governing the instrumental case include:

между	between
перед	in front of
над	over
под	under (location)
за	behind (location)

6. The prepositional or locative case indicates location and is also used when speaking about something or someone. The prepositions most frequently used with this case are:

в	in
на	on
о	about
при	in the presence of

5. Declension of Nouns

Masculine Singular

	Hard		Soft	
	Animate	Inanimate	Animate	Inanimate
Nom.	студе́нт	вопро́с	жи́тел-ь	сара́-й
Gen.	студе́нт-а	вопро́с-а	жи́тел-я	сара́-я
Dat.	студе́нт-у	вопро́с-у	жи́тел-ю	сара́-ю
Acc.	студе́нт-а	вопро́с	жи́тел-я	сара́-й
Inst.	студе́нт-ом	вопро́с-ом	жи́тел-ем	сара́-ем
Prep.	о студе́нт-е	о вопро́с-е	о жи́тел-е	о сара́-е

Masculine Plural

Nom.	студе́нты	вопро́с-ы	жи́тел-и	сара́-и
Gen.	студе́нт-ов	вопро́с-ов	жи́тел-ей	сара́-ев

Dat.	студе́нт-ам	вопро́с-ам	жи́тел-ям	сара́-ям
Acc.	студе́нт-ов	вопро́с-ы	жи́тел-ей	сара́-и
Inst.	студе́нт-ами	вопро́с-ами	жи́тел-ями	сара́-ями
Prep.	о студе́нт-ах	о вопро́с-ах	о жи́тел-ях	о сара́-ях

NOTICE

The accusative case of masculine animate nouns is the same as
the genitive, and of inanimate nouns is the same as the nominative.

FEMININE SINGULAR

	Hard	Soft	
Nom.	ко́мнат-а	земля́	семья́
Gen.	ко́мнат-ы	земл-и́	семьи́
Dat.	ко́мнат-е	земл-е́	семь-е́
Acc.	ко́мнат-у	зе́мл-ю	семь-ю́
Inst.	ко́мнат-ой(ою)	земл-ёй	семь-ёй
Prep.	о ко́мнат-е	о земл-е́	о семь-е́

FEMININE PLURAL

	Hard	Soft	
Nom.	ко́мнат-ы	зе́мл-и	се́мь-и
Gen.	ко́мнат	земе́л-ь	сем-е́й
Dat.	ко́мнат-ам	зе́мл-ям	се́мь-ям
Acc.	ко́мнат-ы	зе́мл-и	се́мь-и́
Inst.	ко́мнат-ами	зе́мл-ями	се́мь-ями
Prep.	о ко́мнат-ах	о зе́мл-ях	о се́мь-ях

NEUTER SINGULAR

	Hard	Soft	
Nom.	окно́	мо́ре	жела́ние
Gen.	окн-а́	мо́р-я	жела́н-ия
Dat.	окн-у́	мо́р-ю	жела́н-ию
Acc.	окн-о́	мо́р-е	жела́н-ие
Inst.	окн-о́м	мо́р-ем	жела́н-ием
Prep.	об[1] окн-е́	о мо́р-е	о жела́н-ии

[1] б is added to the preposition here for the sake of euphony.

NEUTER PLURAL

	Hard	Soft	
Nom.	о́кн-а	мор-я́	жела́н-ия
Gen.	о́к-он	мор-е́й	жела́н-ий
Dat.	о́кн-ам	мор-я́м	жела́н-иям
Acc.	о́кн-а	мор-я́	жела́н-ия
Inst.	о́кн-ами	мор-я́ми	жела́н-иями
Prep.	об[1] о́кн-ах	о мор-я́х	о жела́н-ия

SOME IRREGULAR DECLENSIONS

	MASC.	FEMININE		NEUTER	

SINGULAR

	MASC.	FEMININE		NEUTER	
Nom.	путь	мать	дочь	и́мя	дитя́
Gen.	пут-и́	ма́т-ери	до́ч-ери	и́м-ени	дит-я́ти[2]
Dat.	пут-и́	ма́т-ери	до́ч-ери	и́м-ени	дит-я́ти[2]
Acc.	путь	ма́ть	до́чь	и́мя	дитя́
Inst.	пут-ём	ма́т-ерью	до́ч-ерью	и́м-енем	дит-я́тей[2]
Prep.	о пут-и́	о ма́т-ери	о до́ч-ери	об и́м-ени	о дит-я́ти[2]

PLURAL

	MASC.	FEMININE		NEUTER	
Nom.	пут-и́	ма́т-ери	до́ч-ери	им-ена́	де́т-и
Gen.	пут-е́й	мат-ере́й	доч-ере́й	им-ён	дет-е́й
Dat.	пут-я́м	мат-еря́м	доч-еря́м	им-ена́м	де́т-ям
Acc.	пут-и́	мат-ере́й	доч-ере́й	им-ена́	дет-е́й[3]
Inst.	пут-я́ми	мат-еря́ми	доч-ерьми́	им-ена́ми	дет-ьми́
Prep.	о пут-я́х	о мат-еря́х	о доч-еря́х	об им-ена́х	о де́т-ях

---

[1] б is added to the preposition here for the sake of euphony.

[2] Old form, seldom used.

[3] Accusative case of animate neuter nouns is same as the genitive.

6. Declension of Adjectives

Singular

Masc.	Fem.	Neut.	Masc.	Fem.	Neut.
ый	ая	ое	ой	ая	ое
Nom.					
но́вый	но́вая	но́вое	сухо́й	суха́я	сухо́е
Gen.					
но́в-ого	но́в-ой	но́в-ого	сух-о́го	сух-о́й	сух-о́го
Dat.					
но́в-ому	но́в-ой	но́в-ому	сух-о́му	сух-о́й	сух-о́му
Acc.					
Same as nom. or gen.	но́в-ую	но́в-ое	Same as nom. or gen.	сух-у́ю	сух-о́е
Inst.					
но́в-ым	но́в-ой	но́в-ым	сух-и́м	сух-о́й	сух-и́м
Prep.					
о но́в-ом	о но́в-ой	о но́в-ом	о сух-о́м	о сухо́й	о сух-о́м

Plural

	Masc.		Fem.	
Nom.	но́в-ые		сух-и́е	
Gen.	но́в-ых		сух-и́х	
Dat.	но́в-ым		сух-и́м	
Acc.	Same as nom. or gen.		Same as nom. or gen.	
Inst.	но́в-ыми		сух-и́ми	
Prep.	о но́в-ых		о сух-и́х	

Singular · Plural

	Masc.	Fem.	Neut.	Plural
Nom.	си́н-ий	си́н-яя	си́н-ее	си́н-ие
Gen.	си́н-его	си́н-ей	си́н-его	си́н-их
Dat.	си́н-ему	си́н-ей	си́н-ему	си́н-им
Acc.	Same as nom. or gen.	си́н-юю	си́н-ее	Same as nom. or gen.
Inst.	си́н-им	си́н-ей	си́н-им	си́н-ими
Prep.	о си́н-ем	о си́н-ей	о си́н-ем	о си́н-их

7. DECLENSION OF PRONOUNS

	SING.	PLUR.	SING.	PLUR. AND POLITE	SING. OR PLUR.
	I	we	you	you	-self
Nom.	я	мы	ты	вы	
Gen.	меня́	нас	тебя́	вас	себя́
Dat.	мне́	нам	тебе	вам	себе́
Acc.	меня́	нас	тебя́	ас	себя́
Inst.	мно́й	на́ми	тобо́й	ва́ми	собо́й
Prep.	о́бо мне́	о нас	о тебе́	о вас	о себе́

	SINGULAR			PLURAL
	he	she	it	All genders they
Nom.	он	она́	оно́	они́
Gen.	его́	её	его́	их
Dat.	ему́	ей	ему́	им
Acc.	его́	её	его́	их
Inst.	им	е́ю	им	и́ми
Prep.	о нём	о ней	о нём	о них

	SINGULAR my			PLURAL my
	Masc.	Fem.	Neut.	All genders
Nom.	мой	моя́	моё	мои́
Gen.	моего́	мое́й	моего́	мои́х
Dat.	моему́	мое́й	моему́	мои́м
Acc.	Same. as nom. or gen.	мою́	Same as nom. or gen.	Same as nom. or gen.
Inst.	мои́м	мое́й	мои́м	мои́ми
Prep.	о моём	о мое́й	о моём	о мои́х

твой (your, sing.), свой (one's own, their own) are declined in the same way.

For the third-person possessive, the genitive case of the personal pronouns is used. It always agrees with the gender and number of the possessor.

Nominative	Genitive	
он	его́	his
она́	её	her
оно́	его́	its
они́	их	their

	SINGULAR our		Neut.	PLURAL our
	Masc.	Fem.		All genders
Nom.	наш	на́ша	на́ше	на́ши
Gen.	на́ш-его	на́ш-ей	на́ш-его	на́ш-их
Dat.	на́ш-ему	на́ш-ей	на́ш-ему	на́ш-им
Acc.	Same as . nom or . or gen.	наш-у	Same as. nom. gen	Same as nom. or gen.
Inst.	на́ш-им	на́ш-ей	на́ш-им	на́ш-ими
Prep.	о на́ш-ем	о на́ш-ей	о на́ш-ем	о на́ш-их

ваш (your, *plural* or *polite*) is declined in the same way.

	SINGULAR all		Neut.	PLURAL all
	Masc.	Fem.		All genders
Nom.	весь	вся	всё	все
Gen.	вс-его́	вс-ей	всего	всех
Dat.	вс-ему́	вс-ей	вс-ему́	вс-ем
Acc.	Same as nom. or gen.	вс-ю	всё	Same as as nom. or gen.
Inst.	вс-ем	вс-ей	вс-ем	вс-еми
Prep.	обо вс-ём	обо вс-ей	обо вс-ём	обо вс-ех

	Singular this			Plural these
	Masc.	Fem.	Neut.	All genders
Nom.	э́тот	э́та	э́то	э́ти
Gen.	э́т-ого	э́т-ой	э́т-ого	э́т-их
Dat.	э́т-ому	э́т-ой	э́т-ому	э́т-им
Acc.	Same as nom. or gen.	э́т-у	э́то	Same as nom. or gen.
Inst.	э́т-им	э́т-ой	э́т-им	э́т-ими
Prep.	об э́т-ом	об э́т-ой	об э́т-ом	об э́т-их

	Singular that			Plural those
	Masc.	Fem.	Neut.	All genders
Nom.	тот	та	то	те
Gen.	т-ого́	т-ой	т-ого́	т-ех
Dat.	т-ому́	т-ой	т-ому́	т-ем
Acc.	Same as nom. or gen.	т-у	т-о	Same as nom. or gen.
Inst.	т-ем	т-ой	т-ем	т-е́ми
Prep.	о т-ом	о т-ой	о т-ом	о т-ех

	Singular oneself			Plural themselves
	Masc.	Fem.	Neut.	All genders
Nom.	сам	сама́	само́	са́ми
Gen.	сам-ого́	сам-о́й	сам-ого́	сам-и́х
Dat.	сам-ому́	сам-о́й	сам-ому́	сам-и́м
Acc.	сам-ого́	сам-оё	сам-о́	сам-и́х
Inst.	сам-и́м	сам-о́й	сам-и́м	сам-и́ми
Prep.	о сам-о́м	о сам-о́й	о сам-о́м	о сам-и́х

	Singular Whose			Plural
	Masc.	Fem.	Neut.	All genders
Nom.	чей	чья	чьё	чьи
Gen.	чьего́	чьей	чьего́	чьих
Dat.	чьему́	чьей	чьему́	чьим
Acc.	чей or чьего́	чью	чьё	чьи or чьих
Inst.	чьим	чьей	чьим	чьи́ми
Prep.	о чьём	о чьей	о чьём	о чьих

8. COMPARATIVE OF ADJECTIVES

To form the comparative of an adjective, drop the gender ending and add **ee** for all genders and the plural, as well. The adjective does not decline in the comparative:

краси́вый	pretty
краси́в-ее	prettier
тёплый	warm
тепл-её	warmer
весёлый	merry
весел-ёе	merrier

IRREGULAR COMPARATIVE FORMS

хоро́ший	good
лу́чше	better
большо́й	big
бо́льше	bigger
ма́ленький	small
ме́ньше	smaller
широ́кий	wide
ши́ре	wider
у́зкий	narrow
у́же	narrower
плохо́й	bad
ху́же	worse
высо́кий	tall
вы́ше	taller
ти́хий	quiet
ти́ше	quieter
дорого́й	dear
доро́же	dearer
просто́й	simple
про́ще	simpler

| то́лстый | fat |
| то́лще | fatter |

9. SUPERLATIVE OF ADJECTIVES

The superlative of adjectives has two forms. The simpler form makes use of the word **са́мый**, **са́мая**, **са́мое**, **са́мые** (the most):

са́мый большо́й	the biggest
са́мая краси́вая	the prettiest
са́мый умный	the most clever

The word **са́мый** declines with the adjective:

в са́мом большо́м до́ме
in the very largest house.

Он пришёл с са́мой краси́вой же́нщиной.
He came with the prettiest woman.

10. CASES USED WITH CARDINAL NUMERALS

оди́н (*m.*), одна́ (*f.*), одно́ (*n.*), одни́ (*pl.*)
два (*m.*), две (*f.*), два (*n.*)

A. When the number is used in the nominative case:

after **оди́н**, **одна́**, **одно́**–use the nominative
  singular.
after **одни́**–use the nominative *plural.*
after **два**, **две**, **три**, **четы́ре**–use the genitive
  singular.
after **пять**, **шесть**, **семь**, etc.–use the genitive
  plural.

B. When the number is compound, the case of the noun depends on the last digit:

два́дцать оди́н каранда́ш (nominative *singular*)
twenty-one pencils
два́дцать два карандаша́ (genitive *singular*)
twenty-two pencils
два́дцать пять карандаше́й (genitive *plural*)
twenty-five pencils

11. DECLENSION OF CARDINAL NUMERALS

All cardinal numerals decline, agreeing in case with the noun they modify (with the exception of the nominative case, discussed above).

Я оста́лся без одно́й копе́йки. (genitive
  singular)
I was left without one cent.

Он был там оди́н ме́сяц без двух дней.
  (genitive plural)
He was there one month less two days.

Мы пришли́ к пяти́ часа́м. (dative *plural*)
  We arrived about five o'clock.

Они говоря́т о семи́ рубля́х. (prepositional
  plural)
They are speaking about seven rubles.

TABLE OF DECLENSION OF NUMERALS

	ONE			TWO	THREE	FOUR
	Singular		Plural.			
	Masc., Neut.	Fem.		Masc., Fem.		
Nom.	один, одно́	одна́	одни́	две	три	четы́ре
Gen.	одного́	одно́й	одни́х	двух	трёх	четырёх
Dat.	одному́	одно́й	одни́м	двум	трём	четырём
Acc.	оди́н, одно́	одну́	одни́	два, две	три	четы́ре
	одного́		одни́х	двух	трёх	четырёх
Inst.	одни́м	одно́й	одни́ми	двумя́	тремя́	четырьмя́
Prep.	об одно́м	об одно́й	об одни́х	о двух	о трёх	о четырёх

	FIVE	SIX	SEVEN	EIGHT	NINE	TEN
Nom.	пять	шесть	семь	во́семь	де́вять	де́сять
Gen.	пяти́	шести́	семи́	восьми́	девяти́	десяти́
Dat.	пяти́	шести́	семи́	восьми́	девяти́	десяти́
Acc.	пять	шесть	семь	во́семь	де́вять	де́сять
Inst.	пятью́	шестью́	семью́	восьмью́	девятью́	десятью́
Prep.	о пяти́	о шести́	о семи́	о восьми́	о девяти́	о десяти́

12. ORDINAL NUMERALS

All ordinal numerals are like adjectives, and decline the same as adjectives:

MASC.	FEM.	NEUT.	PLURAL
			(all genders)
пе́рвый	пе́рвая	пе́рвое	пе́рвые
второ́й	втора́я	второ́е	вторы́е

When they are compound, only the last digit changes its form, and only that digit is declined.

двадца́тый век	twentieth century
Э́то бы́ло три́дцать пе́рвого декабря́.	That was on December 31.

тре́тий раз	third time

Втора́я мирова́я война́ ко́нчилась в ты́сяча девятьсо́т со́рок пя́том году́.	The Second World War ended in 1945 (one thousand, nine hundred, forty fifth year).
пя́тый год	
пя́том году́	(prepositional singular)

13. DOUBLE NEGATIVES

With words such as:

ничего́	nothing
никто́	nobody
никогда́	never
никуда́	nowhere

a second negative must be used:

I	nothing	don't	(verb)
Я	ничего́	не	хочу́, зна́ю.

Nobody		don't	(verb)
Никто́		не	ви́дит, говори́т

Never		don't	(verb)
Он никогда́		не	был в Москве́.
Мы никогда́		не	говори́м по-ру́сски.

A negative adverb or pronoun must use a negative with the verb it modifies. (For more on negative expressions, see pages 14-15.)

14. VERBS

Russian verbs have two conjugations. Infinitives of most verbs belonging to the first conjugation end with -ать or -ять. Infinitives of verbs belonging to the second conjugation end with -еть or -ить. Although this is true of a great body of Russian verbs, there are many exceptions, several of which are included in this summary.

A. TYPICAL CONJUGATIONS OF IMPERFECTIVE VERBS:

FIRST CONJUGATION
чита́ть to read

Present Tense:
> я чита́ю
> ты чита́ешь
> он чита́ет
> мы чита́ем
> вы чита́ете
> они́ чита́ют

Past Tense:	чита́л (*m.*)
	чита́ла (*f.*)
	чита́ло (*n.*)
	чита́ли (*pl.*)

Future Tense:	я бу́ду
	ты бу́дешь
	он бу́дет
	мы бу́дем	чита́ть
	вы бу́дете
	они́ бу́дут

Conditional:	чита́л бы
	чита́ла бы
	чита́ло бы
	чита́ли бы

| Imperative: | чита́й |
| | чита́йте |

Participles:

Active:
| Present Tense: | чита́ющий |
| Past Tense: | чита́вший |

Passive:
| Present Tense: | чита́емый |
| Past Tense: | чи́танный |

Gerund:

| Present Tense: | чита́я |
| Past Tense: | прочита́в |

SECOND CONJUGATION

говори́ть
to speak

Present Tense: **я говорю́**
ты говори́шь
он говори́т
они говоря́т
мы говори́м
вы говори́те
они говоря́т

Past Tense: **говори́л** *(m.)*
говори́ла *(f.)*
говори́ло *(n.)*
говори́ли *(pl.)*

Future Tense: **я буду**
ты бу́дешь
он бу́дет
мы бу́дем } **говори́ть**
вы бу́дете
они бу́дут

Conditional: **говори́л бы**
говори́ла бы
говори́ло бы
говори́ли бы

Imperative: **говори́**
говори́те

Participles:

Present Tense:	**говоря́щий**
Past Tense:	**говори́вший**

Gerund:

Present Tense:	**говоря́**
Past Tense:	**сказа́в**

(formed from the perfective verb **сказа́ть**–to tell)

B. MIXED CONJUGATION–PRESENT TENSE

хоте́ть
to want

я хочу́	мы хоти́м
ты хо́чешь	вы хоти́те
он хо́чет	они хотя́т

NOTICE

This verb in the singular has first conjugation endings, with the т changing to ч. In the plural it has second-conjugation endings. The past tense is regular.

C. REFLEXIVE VERBS:

Verbs ending with -ся or -сь are reflexive. Ся usually follows a consonant, and сь a vowel. These verbs follow the general form of conjugation, regaining the endings -ся after consonants and -сь after vowels.

заниматься
to study

я занима́юсь	мы занима́емся
ты занима́ешься	вы занима́етесь
он занима́ется	они́ занима́ются

D. The verb "to be"

The verb "to be" (**быть**) is usually omitted in the present tense, but is used in the past tense:

был (*m.*)
была́ (*f.*)
бы́ло (*n.*)
бы́ли (*pl.*)

and in the future tense:

я бу́ду	мы бу́дем
ты бу́дешь	вы бу́дете
он бу́дет	они́ бу́дут

It is also used as an auxiliary verb in the imperfective future.

E. Conjugations of some irregular verbs in the present tense:

брать to take

я беру́	мы берём
ты берёшь	вы берёте
он берёт	они́ беру́т

вести́ to lead

я веду́	мы ведём
ты ведёшь	вы ведёте
он ведёт	они веду́т

жить to live

я живу́	мы живём
ты живёшь	вы живёте
он живёт	они живу́т

звать to call

я зову́	мы зовём
ты зовёшь	вы зовёте
он зовёт	они зову́т

нести́ to carry

я несу́	мы несём
ты несёшь	вы несёте
он несёт	они несу́т

дава́ть to give

я даю́	мы даём
ты даёшь	вы даёте
он даёт	они даю́т

F. Conjugations of irregular perfective verbs—perfective future:

дать to give

я дам	мы дади́м
ты дашь	вы дади́те
он даст	они даду́т

сесть   to sit down

я ся́ду	мы ся́дем
ты ся́дешь	вы ся́дете
он ся́дет	они́ ся́дут

G. Perfective and Imperfective Aspects of a Verb:

Russian verbs can be perfective or imperfective. Imperfective verbs express continuous action. They have three tenses: past, present, and future. Perfective verbs indicate completion of action, beginning of action, or both, and have only two tenses: past and future.

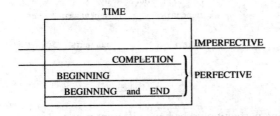

Some perfective verbs are formed by adding the prefixes **с, на, вы, в, по,** etc., to imperfective verbs. When a prefix is added to a verb, not only is the perfective formed, but very often the meaning of the verb is changed at the same time.

Imperfective	Perfective
писа́ть to write	**написа́ть** to write down
	переписа́ть to copy

When the meaning of the verb changes, the new verb **переписать** (to copy) that has been formed must have its own imperfective. To form the imperfective of such new forms, the suffix **ыв, ив**, or **ав** is added:

IMPERFECTIVE	PERFECTIVE	IMPERFECTIVE
		перепи́сывать
		to copy
чита́ть to read	прочита́ть	прочи́тывать
	to finish reading or to read through	
	перечита́ть	перечи́тывать
	to read over	
знать to know	узна́ть	узнава́ть
	to find out or to recognize	
дава́ть to give	дать to give	
	отда́ть	отдава́ть
	to give out or away	
	переда́ть	передава́ть
	to pass	
	зада́ть	задава́ть
	to assign	
	сдать	сдава́ть
	to deal cards	

Some perfective verbs have different roots:

говори́ть to speak	сказа́ть to tell	
	заговори́ть	загова́ривать
	to begin talking	
	рассказа́ть	расска́зывать
	to tell a story	
	заказа́ть	зака́зывать
	to order something	
	to be made or done	
	приказа́ть	прика́зывать
	to order, to command	

Prefixes can be added to either **говори́ть** or **сказа́ть**, but each addition makes a new verb; e.g.:

за-говори́ть	to begin talking
за-каза́ть	to order something
от-говори́ть	to talk someone out of something
(от-гова́ривать)	
рассказа́ть	to tell a story

The past tense of the perfective verb is formed in the same way as the past tense of the imperfective verb.

H. FUTURE TENSE

The future tense has two forms: imperfective future and perfective future. As has already been pointed out, the imperfective future is formed by using the auxiliary verb **быть** with the infinitive of the imperfective verb:

я бу́ду		I will	
ты бу́дешь		you will	
он бу́дет	говори́ть, чита́ть,	he will	speak, read,
мы бу́дем	понима́ть, etc.	we will	understand, etc.
вы бу́дете		you will	
они́ бу́дут		they will	

The perfective future is formed without using the auxiliary verb **быть**:

PRESENT		PERFECTIVE FUTURE	
Я пишу́	I write	я напишу́	I will write
ты говори́шь	you speak	ты ска́жешь	you will say
он идёт	he goes	он придёт	he will come
мы чита́ем	we read	мы прочита́ем	we will read (it)

Present		Perfective Future	
вы смо́трите	you look	вы посмо́трите	you will look
они́ е́дут	they go	они́ прие́дут	they will come
	[ride]		[riding]

NOTICE

The perfective verb is conjugated the same as the imperfective verb.

I. Verbs of motion

Verbs of motion have many variations of meaning. A different verb is used to express movement by an outside agency or instrument than is used to express movement by foot.

Each of these verbs (i.e., indicating movement by foot or movement by conveyance) has two forms: one describes a single action in one direction, and the other, a repeated action. All of these forms are imperfective. The perfective is formed by adding a prefix to a single-action verb. But bear in mind that the addition of the prefix changes the meaning of the verb. The same prefix affixed to the repeated-action verb forms the imperfective of the new verb.

Imperfective	Repeated Action	One Action		Perfective
	ходи́ть	идти́	to go on foot	
	е́здить	е́хать	to go by vehicle	
выходи́ть			to go out on foot	вы́йти
выезжа́ть			to go out by vehicle	вы́ехать
приходи́ть			to come on foot [arrive]	прийти́
приезжа́ть			to come by vehicle [arrive]	прие́хать
заходи́ть			to drop in [visit] on foot	зайти́
заезжа́ть			to drop in [visit] by vehicle	зае́хать
находи́ть			to find	найти́
	носи́ть	нести́	to carry on foot	
	вози́ть	везти́	to carry by vehicle	
приноси́ть			to bring on foot	принести́
привози́ть			to bring by vehicle	привезти́

идти́
to go on foot
(single action in one direction)

PRESENT TENSE	PAST TENSE
я иду́	
ты идёшь	
он идёт	он шёл
мы идём	она шла
вы идёте	оно шло
они иду́т	они шли

ходи́ть
to go on foot
(repeated action)

PRESENT TENSE	PAST TENSE
я хожу́	Regular
ты хо́дишь	
он хо́дит	
мы хо́дим	
вы хо́дите	
они хо́дят	

е́хать
to go by vehicle
(single action in one direction)

PRESENT TENSE	PAST TENSE
я е́ду	Regular
ты едешь	
он е́дет	
мы е́дем	
вы е́дете	
они́ е́дут	

е́здить
to go by vehicle
(repeated action)

PRESENT TENSE	PAST TENSE
я е́зжу	Regular
ты е́здишь	
он е́здит	
мы е́здим	
вы е́здите	
они е́здят	

нести́
to carry on foot
(single action in one direction)

PRESENT TENSE	PAST TENSE
я несу́	мы несли́
ты несёшь	вы несли
он несёт	он нёс
мы несём	она несла
вы несёте	оно несло́
они несу́т	они несли

носи́ть
to carry on foot
(repeated action)

PRESENT TENSE	PAST TENSE
я ношу́	Regular
ты но́сишь	
он но́сит	
мы но́сим	
вы но́сить	
они но́сят	

везти́

to carry by vehicle

(single action in one direction)

PRESENT TENSE	PAST TENSE
я везу́	
ты везёшь	
он везёт	он вёз
мы везём	она́ везла́
вы везёте	оно́ везло
они́ везу́т	они́ везли́

вози́ть

to carry by vehicle

(repeated action)

PRESENT TENSE	PAST TENSE
я вожу́	Regular
ты во́зишь	
он во́зит	
мы во́зим	
вы во́зите	
они́ во́зят	

J. SUBJUNCTIVE AND CONDITIONAL MOODS

The formation of the subjunctive and conditional in many languages constitutes one of the most difficult grammatical constructions. However, in Russian this is one of the easiest. To form the subjunctive or conditional, the past tense of the verb is used after the particle **бы**:

е́сли бы   if

Е́сли бы я знал, } If I knew,
Had I known,

я пошёл бы. } I would have gone.

I would go.

Я позвони́л бы,   I would have called you,
éсли бы у меня́   if I had your tele-
был ваш но́мер   phone number

K. IMPERATIVE MOOD

The imperative mood of a verb (see page 171) is formed from the second-person singular, present tense. For the singular imperative, replace the ending with -и, -й, or -ь. For the plural imperative, add -те to the singular:

INFINITIVE	SECOND-PERSON SINGULAR	FAMILIAR, SINGULAR	PLURAL, POLITE
писа́ть	пи́ш-ешь	пиши́!	пиши́те!
to write		Write!	
повторя́ть	повторя́-ешь	повторя́й!	повторя́йте!
to repeat		Repeat!	
броса́ть	броса́-ешь	брось!	броса́йте!
to throw		Throw!	
рабо́тать	рабо́та-ешь	рабо́тай!	рабо́тайте!
to work		Work!	
чита́ть	чита́-ешь	чита́й!	чита́йте!
to read		Read!	

The reflexive verb retains its endings (**ся** after a consonant or **й**, and **сь** after a vowel):

мы́ться	мо́-ешься	мо́йся!	мо́йтесь!
to wash (oneself)			
занима́ться	занима́ешься	занима́йся!	занима́йтесь!
to study			

In giving an order indirectly to a third person, the forms **пусть** and **пуска́й** are used with the third person singular:

Пусть он чита́ет.   Let him read. (He should read.)
Пуска́й она́ говори́т.   Let her speak. (She should speak.)

L. PARTICIPLES AND GERUNDS

Participles and gerunds are very important parts of the Russian language, so it is necessary to know how to recognize them and to understand them. However, it should be made clear that they are not used very much in simple conversation, but rather in literature and scientific writing.

Participles are verb-adjective; gerunds are verb-adverbs. Participles are adjectives made out of verbs. The difference between an adjective and a participle is in tense; i.e., participles can be present or past tense, active or passive voice. They retain this verb quality; but in every other respect they are adjectives. They have three genders: masculine, feminine, and neuter. They decline the same as adjectives and agree with the words they modify in gender, case, and number.

	Present	Past
Говори́ть	говоря́щий, ая, ее, ие	говори́вший, ая, ее, ие

PREPOSITIONAL PLURAL:

Мы говори́м о говоря́щих по-англи́йски учени́ка́х.
We are talking about students who speak English.

Gerunds are verb-adverbs and as such do not change, but have present and past tense. The present tense is formed from the imperfective; the past tense must be formed from the perfective. The present tense is characterized by two actions that take place at the same time. In the past tense, one action follows the other; when the first action is completed, the second one starts.

Present tense:

читать   **Читая, он улыбался.**
              While reading, he was smiling
              (two simultaneous actions).

Past tense:

прочитать   **Прочитав газету, он встал и
              ушёл.**
              Having finished reading the
              paper, he got up and went away
              (one action following the other).

LETTER WRITING

A. A NOTE ON LETTER WRITING

Both in formal and informal writing, the adressee's name, title, and postal adress appear only on the envelope. In formal letters, an istitution's name and adress often appear at the top of the document, while the date is found at the bottom of the page.

Since the demise of the Soviet Union, the form of address in formal writing has changed. Instead of writing to a "comrade" (товарищ), Russians now write to Mr. or Mrs. (господин, госпожа). The abbreviated forms are г-н (or simply г.) for Mr. and г-жа for Mrs. In formal writing the use of a title is common, and if one wants to write to editorial offices of newspapers or journals, the phrase "Dear editorial board" (Уважаемая редакция) is commonly used.

The abbreviated form of the date differs from the one used in the United States. December 20, 1992, for example, is written as 20-12-92 or as 20/XII/92. Address writing is different as well. Russians begin with the city, then write the street and house number, then apartment number, then the name of the addressee (in dative case).

B. BUSINESS LETTERS

г. Москва 157332
Ул. Петрова, д. 8
Всероссийское издательство Наука
Отдел по международным связям

Уважаемый г. Степанов!

Мы получили Ваш заказ на доставку последних номеров журнала «Континент». К сожалению, в связи с повышением почтовых тарифов, мы не смогли отправить заказ вовремя. Доставка журналов ожидается в первых числах ноября.

С уважением,
Г. И. Аполлонов
Директор отдела по
международным связям.

12 октября 1992
г. Москва

Moskva 157332
Petrova 8
All-Russian publishing house Science
Section on foreign affairs

Dear Mr. Stepanov,

We have received your order to deliver the latest issues of the journal "Kontinent." Unfortunately, due to the increases in postal tariffs, we could not send you your order on time. The delivery of the issues is expected in early November.

Sincerely,
G. I. Apollonov
Director of the Section on
foreign affairs

October 12, 1992
Moscow

г. Москва 122771
Ул. Васнецова, д. 2
Совместное предприятие «Роза»

Уважаемый г. Кожинов!

Отвечаем на Ваш запрос о возможности установить
торговые связи с Германией. К сожалению, в настоящее
время мы не в состоянии помочь Вам в этом деле.
Наше предприятие не уполномочено действовать
посредниками между западными и русскими фирмами.

С уважением,
Н. И. Сошников
Директор предприятия

13/XI/92
г. Москва

Moskva 122771
Vasnetsova St. 2
Joint Venture "Rose"

Dear Mr. Kozhinov,

This is in response to your inquiry about the possibility of estab-
lishing trade contacts with Germany. Unfortunately, we are unable
to help you at present. Our business is not authorized to act as medi-
ators between Western and Russian firms.

Sincerely,
N. I. Soshnikov
Director of the firm

November 13, 1992
Moscow

C. INFORMAL LETTERS

27-10-92

Дорогой Иван!

Наконец, приехал в Псков. С билетами было трудно,
но, в конце концов, Ирина достала и даже на скорый
поезд. В общем, могу взяться за работу. Директор
нашёл неплохую квартиру. Наверное, действительно
хотят, чтобы мне было удобно. Жалко, что не успели
поговорить в Москве, но в ноябре собираюсь приехать
и, конечно, позвоню.

Скучаю по московским друзьям. Не забывай. Пиши!

Твой Сергей.

10-27-92

Dear Ivan,

I have finally arrived in Pskov. There was difficulty with the
tickets, but in the end Irina managed to get them and even for
an express train. So, I can get down to work. The director
found a decent apartment. It seems they really want to make me
comfortable. Too bad we didn't have time to talk in Moscow,
but I plan to come in November and will call you of course.

I miss my Moscow friends. Don't forget me. Write!

Your Sergei.

17-11-92

Дорогая Наташа!

Давно уже не получаю от тебя писем и очень
беспокоюсь о родителях. Как здоровье отца?
Собирается мама уходить на пенсию или опять
откладывает? Позвони мне на работу, домашний
телефон ещё не подключили.
Девочки растут, Марина пошла в первый класс и очень
гордится. Таня даёт ей советы.
Все у нас хорошо. Миша передаёт привет. Надеюсь
увидеть всех вас на праздники.

Целую,
Ваша Галя.

11-17-92

Dear Natasha,

I have not received letters from you in a while and I worry a
lot about our parents. How is father's health? Is Mom going to
retire or is she delaying again? Call me at work: our home
phone has not yet been connected.
The girls are growing. Marina started first grade and is very
proud. Tania gives her advice.
Everything is fine with us. Misha sends regards. I hope to see
you for the holidays.

Kisses,
Your Galia.

D. FORM OF THE ENVELOPE

addressee
sender

1. Business Letters

г. Москва 332889
ул. Страхова, д.5, кв.75
Павлову Ивану Петровичу

г. Псков 32435
ул. Надеждина, д.4,кв. 11
Сергей Суриков

Moscow 332889
Strakhova St. 5, apt.75
Pavlov, Ivan Petrovich

Pskov 32435
Nadezhdina St. 4, apt. 11
Sergei Surikov

2. Informal Letters

г. Ставрополь 32456
ул. Кураева, д.1, кв.75
Семеновой Наталье Ивановне

г. Новосибирск 30897
ул. Королёва, д.15, кв. 33
Г.И. Синицына

Stavropol 32456
Kuraeva 1, apt.75
Semenova Natalia Ivanovna

Novosibirsk 30897
Koroleva 15, apt.33
Sinitsina G.I.

NOTES